PRACTICING THE WRITING PROCESS 4
THE WRITING TEST

BY
SHEILA C. CROWELL
&
ELLEN D. KOLBA

EDUCATIONAL DESIGN, INC. **EDI 258**

ISBN# 0-87694-400-4   EDI 258

TABLE OF CONTENTS

▲ *UNIT TWO: Writing About Advantages and Disadvantages*

ESSAY TOPIC: A SCHOOL DRESS CODE

ESSAY TOPIC: SUMMER SCHOOL

ESSAY TOPIC: FAST FOOD

ESSAY TOPIC: VOLUNTEER WORK

▲ *UNIT THREE: The Problem-Solution Essay*

ESSAY TOPIC: FOOD SERVICE OPTIONS AT SCHOOL

ESSAY TOPIC: COMMUNITY VOLUNTEER WORK OPTIONS

▲ *UNIT FOUR: The How-To Essay*

ESSAY TOPIC: YOUR PET "TRADE SECRET"

▲ *UNIT FIVE: The Descriptive Essay*

ESSAY TOPIC: AN EXTRACURRICULAR ACTIVITY

PART TWO: SENTENCE CONSTRUCTION, USAGE, AND MECHANICS

PART THREE: PRACTICE TESTS

ANSWER KEYS

TO THE TEACHER

In recent years many state and municipal school systems have instituted mandatory writing tests. These tests typically require all students at a given grade level to produce a writing sample on an assigned topic. The tests also often contain a multiple-choice component that tests students on their knowledge of sentence construction, grammar, usage, and mechanics (spelling, punctuation, and capitalization).

Practicing the Writing Process 4: The Writing Test is designed to help students prepare for writing tests like these. *Part One* shows students how to produce a successful essay in response to a variety of typical "prompts," or assigned topics. *Part Two* is a handy review of the major points of sentence construction, grammar, usage, spelling, punctuation, and capitalization that are most frequently found on writing tests. *Part Three* consists of tests on the material covered in *Part Two*.

In addition, *The Writing Test* is designed to help students become better writers in general. The kinds of writing assessed on the tests are ones that are required in school and other academic writing, as well as in the job and business world. Students who can write well-conceived and well-executed essays for tests can usually write them in all circumstances.

The essay asked for by the majority of these tests is usually a variant of the persuasive essay, in which students are asked to take a position on some issue and to give convincing reasons for their opinion. Other tests may ask students to write essays in which they consider the advantages and disadvantages of some situation or course of action, or to write a problem-solution essay, or a "how-to" essays, or even a descriptive essay. All these types of essays are covered in this book, with emphasis being given to the persuasive essay as the essay type demanded most frequently.

This book helps students become better writers (and better test-takers) by concentrating on two things: critical thinking and the revision process. Special sections on thinking skills give students practice in anticipating the consequences of a proposed course of action, in distinguishing facts from opinions, in supporting their opinions with relevant facts and examples, and in using persuasive but unbiased language in presenting their own and opposing points of view.

Research into the writing process indicates that having students revise existing essays—either written by others or by themselves—is one of the best ways to improve their writing skills. The book gives students practice in improving their writing by guiding them in revising a series of model essays that range in competence from well below average to well above average, before having them write essays of their own.

Use the book flexibly, according to your students' needs and in line with the suggestions in the Teachers' Guide.

PART ONE

HOW TO WRITE A SUCCESSFUL ESSAY

PART ONE
INTRODUCTION

This book is designed to help you write better. It will help you write better in school, in real life, and on writing tests.

What Makes a Good Essay?

No matter who reads and responds to your writing—a test grader, teacher, a friend, the editor of a magazine or newspaper—he or she will look for the following things. These are the elements that help you communicate effectively and make your writing succeed. Keep them in mind as you write.

▲ Elaboration and Support

Support and elaboration are perhaps the most important things that readers look for.

Elaboration means developing each of your ideas fully. You can use facts or examples, definitions, descriptions, comparisons, explanations, figurative language, dialogue, quotations, or personal experiences.

Support is the kind of elaboration you need in persuasive writing. It means giving convincing reasons for your position. A convincing reason is one that is relevant to the position you have taken, makes a strong point, and is accurate. It is usually a good idea to have at least two reasons, both of which are elaborated, or developed, as completely as possible.

When you write your own essay, make sure that you have enough support and elaboration for your ideas.

▲ Organization

Organization means arranging things in an order that makes sense. This means all of the following:

Paragraphing—that is, putting each main idea in a paragraph of its own, along with the facts and examples you use to elaborate that idea.

No digressions—that is, no wandering off the subject and including information on other topics.

Transitions—that is, using special words and phrases to show the connections between ideas and to make the organization of the composition clear to the reader. Some common transition words are: *although, because, in addition, finally, however, but, also, too,* etc.

▲ Language Control

Language control means expressing yourself effectively, clearly, and correctly. Readers look for the following:

Well-constructed sentences. Sentences should be constructed so that they are interesting and make sense to the reader.

Varied and correct word choice.

Few errors in spelling, usage, and punctuation.

▲ Awareness of Audience

This means always remembering that you are writing for someone else. While your meaning may be perfectly clear to you, you have to explain things fully and clearly so that someone else can understand it. Readers look for the following:

Following directions. If you are writing for a school assignment or test, you must be careful to follow the directions given about who your audience is. If the question or assignment tells you to write a letter to the editor, make sure your essay is in the form of a letter to the editor.

Appropriate language. No matter who your audience is, relatively formal language is the safest choice. Even if the question or assignment asks you to write a letter to a friend, don't use slang.

▲ Persuasive Purpose

This is a special characteristic that readers look for in a persuasive essay. Persuasive purpose means that anyone who reads your essay knows what you are writing about and what position you take on the subject. Everything should be chosen to convince your reader: the reasons you give, the support you provide, the language you use to express yourself, the organizational pattern you use.

How Are Essays Graded?

Teachers and other people who grade or score essays use different systems for indicating the grades. Some mark papers A, B, C, and so on. Some use a numbering system that starts at 100 and goes down to 0. Some number from 10 down to 1 or 1 up to 10. Some use a scale that goes from 0 to 5 or from 1 to 6. Whatever the system of marking, though, most readers use the following measures to decide whether a paper is great, just average, or below average.

- **At the LOW end of the scale, or BELOW AVERAGE**

  These are essays that are unsatisfactory or only minimally satisfactory. An essay in this category is often too short to contain much information. It doesn't deal with the topic fully or provide sufficient detail, and it may repeat itself. Its organization may be weak. There may be little or no awareness of who the audience is and what the purpose of the essay is. Finally, the essay may contain awkward word choices, sentences that are difficult to understand, and a large number of errors in spelling and usage.

- **In the MIDDLE of the scale, AVERAGE, or JUST PASSING**

  An average essay displays only a fair degree of organization and elaboration. Its organizational pattern may not be entirely consistent, and some digressions may occur. It may not contain a great many details (although the ones it includes are relevant), and it does not develop the topic fully. It exhibits some control of written language, although there may be problems in spelling, usage, or punctuation. Word choice is good, and ideas are clearly expressed, with some transitions from one to another. There is some sense of audience and of the purpose for which the essay was written.

- **At the HIGH end of the scale, ABOVE AVERAGE, or EXCELLENT**

  An essay in this category is well organized and fully elaborated. It contains sufficient detail to develop the topic convincingly. The entire essay is clear and complete. It has a strong introduction and/or conclusion, and the ideas are clearly expressed, with transitions from one idea to another. There may be a few minor errors in spelling, usage, or punctuation, but on the whole, the essay exhibits excellent word choice and varied sentence structure. It uses persuasive strategies (well-ordered, logical arguments) effectively to appeal to the audience.

UNIT ONE
THE PERSUASIVE ESSAY

The first unit of this book is about a kind of writing people often use in school, on the job, and in everyday life—writing to persuade. In persuasive writing, you make a choice and give good reasons for it. You convince your readers to think or feel the way you do, or to take an action that you recommend.

Persuasive writing can take many forms:

- a letter to the editor of the newspaper, expressing your opinion on a townwide issue

- an essay for school, taking a position on a controversial question in current events

- a report for your boss, suggesting a way to solve a problem in the workplace

- an article for the school newspaper, trying to convince other students to re-cycle bottles and cans

A good persuasive essay shows off your reasoning skills as well as your skill at writing. For this reason, it is one of the most common kinds of essay given in school assignments and on writing tests.

The activities in this unit will help you be a more persuasive writer by showing you how to—

- weigh both sides of a question

- state your position or opinion

- support your position or opinion with good reason

- develop your reasons so that they are convincing

- organize your ideas in a way that makes sense

- express yourself clearly and appropriately

Many of the activities in Unit 1 ask you to analyze and improve essays by other students. Why? When you revise an essay that lacks important elements, you learn a great deal about what makes a good essay. Practice in revision prepares you for writing your own successful essay.

1
Critical Thinking

WAYS OF EXPRESSING AN OPINION

When you write to persuade, you need good **reasons** to support your opinion. The reasons tell your reader why you think the way you do.

You also need **facts** to make your opinion more believable to your reader. The more facts you have to support what you say, the more your reader is inclined to agree with you.

Finally, whenever you can, you should use **examples** from your own experience or the experience of others to show that your belief is based on real life.

Using Reasons, Facts, and Examples

What is this writer's opinion about a new state law requiring motorcycle riders to wear helmets?

> I think everyone who rides a motorcycle should be required to wear a helmet.

You know that the writer agrees with the proposed new law, but you don't know why. If a friend said this to you, you could ask: *What makes you say that?* or *Why do you think so?* Then you would wait to hear the reasons.

Readers ask the same kinds of questions that listeners do, but they have no way of asking the author for his or her reasons. If you want to convince your reader, start by giving a reason that makes sense, as this writer did:

> I think everyone who rides a motorcycle should be required to wear a helmet *because helmets prevent head injuries.*

Then the writer added a fact to elaborate the reason. (When you elaborate an idea or a statement you tell more about it or you use more precise language to help your reader understand exactly what you are saying.)

> I think everyone who rides a motorcycle should be required to wear a helmet because helmets prevent head injuries. *Head injuries are often very serious and can have long-term effects.*

Finally, to be even more convincing, the writer added an example drawn from personal experience.

> I think everyone who rides a motorcycle should be required to wear a helmet because helmets prevent head injuries. Head injuries are often serious and can have long-term effects. *Last spring, my friend Luis was riding behind his brother on their motorcycle. It was raining and they hit an oil patch and went out of control. Luis flew off the motorcycle and landed on his head. He was knocked unconscious and went into a coma.*

▲ *Reasons*

Here are some of the ways we measure whether a reason is good:

1. **It makes good common sense.**

2. **It is necessary.** You have proved that you need it or that it needs to be done.

3. **It meets certain standards of ethics or personal values.** You believe that certain things are right and certain things are wrong and you base your opinions on those beliefs.

4. **It has social value.** Whatever you are suggesting is good or right for most people.

5. **It represents quality.** For example, sports fans support the team they think is the best. Of course, they have to back up their opinion with facts when they talk to fans of other teams.

6. **It doesn't cost much.** What you suggest is either inexpensive or is worth what it costs.

7. **It gives pleasure.** If you think something is worth doing because it's fun, that's OK.

Discuss this list in class. Then add three more ways to describe a good reason.

8. _____

_____

9. _____

_____

10. _____

_____

To state your reasons for disagreeing with something, just add a *no* or *not* to the reasons above. (It doesn't make sense; it isn't necessary, etc.)

EXERCISE 1: Determining Good Reasons

Sets of rules are a part of everyone's life. There are school rules, family rules, and work rules. Choose one of these sets of rules and write it here.

_____

_____

Think about all the individual rules in that set. Is there any one you find particularly hard to follow? Would you like to change it? Write the rule you would like to change in the space below.

_____

_____

Now comes the hard part. First, take a look at the list of Good Reasons that you just worked with. See if you can find two good reasons to change the rule you don't like. (Don't forget the ones you added at the end of the list.)

Write your reasons in the space below. Identify each one with the appropriate number from the Good Reasons list. Be prepared to explain your reasons to the class.

1. _____

   _____? [# _____]

2. _____

   _____? [# _____]

▲ *Facts*

You can begin a persuasive essay with two sentences like these:

> I think that our state should pass a law requiring everyone who rides a motorcycle to wear a helmet. *First of all, statistics show that this state has more motorcycle accidents that any other state.*

In this example, the first sentence states your opinion. The second sentence states a fact that supports your position. Your readers will take you seriously because you have given them a fact to support your opinion.

Here's another way to begin the essay.

> I think that our state should pass a law requiring everyone who rides a motorcycle to wear a helmet. *If every rider wore a helmet, our state would be the safest in the country.*

In this example, the second sentence just gives another opinion. A word like <u>safest</u> makes an alert reader ask questions: How do you measure safety? How can you be sure? What proof do you have?

What is the difference between a fact and an opinion? The most important difference is this: FACTS CAN BE CHECKED OR PROVED. You can look them up in a reference book like a dictionary or an encyclopedia. Or you can call an expert. For example, if you want to know what the chemical formula for water is, you can easily look it up. If you want to know how many accidents your state had last year, call the department of transportation.

Opinions cannot be checked or proved. They are statements of belief. When someone writes a sentence like "Summer is my favorite time of year," you accept that statement as the writer's personal opinion. You won't question that the writer feels this way, but you might expect to read some of the reasons why the writer thinks so.

When you read a sentence like "Sue Quarles is the best basketball player on our school team," you probably won't accept the statement without questioning it. You expect the writer to use statistics or examples to prove the point. You expect to be told how many goals Quarles has scored or to be told stories of spectacular plays Quarles has made against tough opponents.

A believable opinion is based on fact. Be prepared to provide some solid proof based on facts and believable examples when you use the following words in your opinion essay:

best, worst, least, most, good, easy

I think, feel, believe

always, never, none, all

EXERCISE 2: Distinguishing Fact and Opinion

Which statements below contain facts that can be checked? Which statements are opinions that need to be supported by facts? Check the correct box for each statement.

Be prepared to explain your choices.

	FACTS (CAN BE CHECKED)	OPINIONS (NEEDS SUPPORT)
1. Motorcycles are dangerous.	❑	❑
2. There were 150 motorcycle accidents in this state last year.	❑	❑
3. Congress should pass a new gun control law.	❑	❑
4. No smoking is allowed on any domestic airline flights.	❑	❑
5. Students who miss school can never learn enough to pass the exams.	❑	❑
6. The National Rifle Association (NRA) pays for ads to fight gun control laws.	❑	❑
7. I plan to take a course in word processing before I graduate.	❑	❑
8. Forty per cent of the survivors of motorcycle accidents suffer serious head wounds.	❑	❑
9. The best grilled chicken sandwich for your Busy Family is at your local B-Z Family Chicken Hut.	❑	❑
10. Today's B-Z Family Meal package is only $4.95 if you buy a portion of our new Sweet Tooth Fruit Salad.	❑	❑
11. Smoking makes some people cough.	❑	❑
12. A winning football team creates school pride.	❑	❑
13. Students who miss school must make up all their work within a week.	❑	❑

continued . . .

	FACTS (CAN BE CHECKED)	OPINIONS (NEEDS SUPPORT)
14. Working as a volunteer in a children's hospital is one of the most satisfying things I have ever done.	❏	❏
15. Our school cafeteria needs a new menu.	❏	❏
16. Showing community spirit through active volunteer work is part of the East Side High School tradition.	❏	❏
17. Yesterday only fourteen students ate the steamed cabbage that was part of the regular lunch.	❏	❏
18. More people eat in fast food restaurants than in regular restaurants.	❏	❏
19. America's favorite place to dine out with the family is in the local fast food restaurant.	❏	❏
20. Our district's school uniform consists of pants, shirt, and tie for the young men and plaid skirt, white blouse, and jacket for the young women.	❏	❏
21. Students who wear uniforms pay more attention in class and are more serious about their work.	❏	❏
22. Taking extra courses in summer school is not a good idea because students need time off to be themselves without any pressure from teachers.	❏	❏
23. Last summer, 25% of this year's senior class took summer courses in SAT Prep.	❏	❏
24. Seniors improved their SAT scores by 75 points over the scores they got in their junior year.	❏	❏
25. Summer courses in SAT prep are a good way to improve your SAT score.	❏	❏

▲ *Examples*

When you use your own experience or the experience of others as an example, be sure that the incident you have chosen relates directly to the point you are trying to make. Choosing **relevant** examples is an important strategy in presenting a convincing argument. Using an irrelevant example confuses your reader.

Look at these two paragraphs. In both of them the author gives an example of what happened to a friend who rode a motorcycle without wearing a helmet.

> I think everyone who rides a motorcycle should be required to wear a helmet because helmets prevent head injuries. Head injuries are often serious and can have long-term effects. Last spring, my friend Luis was riding behind his brother on their motorcycle. *It was raining and they hit an oil patch and went out of control. Luis flew off the motorcycle and landed on his head. He was knocked unconscious and went into a coma.*

> I think everyone who rides a motorcycle should be required to wear a helmet because helmets prevent head injuries. Head injuries are often very serious and can have long-term effects. Last spring, my friend Luis was riding behind his brother on their motorcycle. *They had an accident and Luis landed on his head and broke his collarbone. The break was so bad that he couldn't play football this season, and now it looks like he won't get that athletic scholarship he was counting on.*

Which injury was the result of not wearing a helmet? Clearly, the head injury. Wearing a helmet would not have prevented the broken collarbone.

We say that the example of the broken collarbone is **not relevant** to the importance of wearing helmets while riding a motorcycle. The writer should drop it or not put so much emphasis on it.

EXERCISE 3: Choosing Relevant Examples

In the first exercise in this chapter, you wrote about a rule that you would like to change. Using your own experience, describe an incident which serves as a good example of the reason you want to change the rule. Then tell your story to a classmate and ask if the example seems relevant.

Avoiding Exaggerations

When you feel deeply about something, it is easy to exaggerate. One way of exaggerating is to jump to far-out conclusions on the basis of one or two examples. Here is how one writer expressed her fear of the power of advertising.

> Advertising makes young people want things they can't afford or that aren't good for them. For example, they make expensive sneakers so popular that young people will rob and kill to get them. These kinds of ads should be stopped.

Do you believe the writer or do you think that she has overstated her case?

EXERCISE 4: Finding Exaggerated Statements

Discuss the paragraph above in class, using the following points to guide you.

- Is the first sentence entirely true? Does advertising always do this?

- Is the second sentence true all of the time, some of the time, once in a while, or not at all?

- Do you agree with the last sentence? What does the writer mean by "these kinds of ads"? Does anyone have the right to stop ads?

In the space below, write the conclusion you came to after the discussion about the paragraph.

_____

_____

Sometimes you are so concerned about convincing your audience that some good action should be started or some bad action should be stopped that you exaggerate the effects of an action.

For example, the world is struggling with the problems of pollution and the destruction of the environment. A student who feels deeply about this issue wants the school to do something to help the environment. He begins his essay this way:

> Our school can do something right now to save the planet. If we switch from using styrofoam cups in the cafeteria to regular glass, we can stop the hole in the ozone layer from getting any larger.

Is it really possible for the actions of one school to save the ozone layer? Probably not. Individual actions by themselves cannot solve enormous problems. Here's a more convincing way of presenting his case.

> Our school can do something right now that will help us all learn to be more aware of our need to protect the atmosphere. If we switch from using styrofoam cups in the cafeteria to regular glass, we won't be adding to the problem. And we'll be educating students to be aware of the choices they must make.

EXERCISE 5: Understanding Effective Revisions

Discuss the two paragraphs in class. Consider the following things:

- Look at the first sentence in each paragraph. Do they mean the same thing? Describe the difference in meaning in the space below.

  _____

  _____

- The second sentence in each paragraph begins the same way, but ends differently. Do you think the revision is stronger or weaker than the original? Write your response.

  _____

  _____

- The writer added a sentence in revision. Does this sentence make the paragraph more or less believable? Write your response.

  _____

  _____

EXERCISE 6: Identifying and Revising Exaggerations

Read the following statements. Identify any problems of exaggeration that you find. Discuss in class ways to revise the statements so that they are more effective and more believable.

1. Restaurants serve their customers too many fatty meals. If you want to live a long time, eat at home.

2. Today, being a good athlete gets you into a college on scholarship, but it doesn't help you get a degree. This is criminal, and athletes should refuse to play for teams that take advantage of them.

3. Schools should forbid students to work after school until senior year. My cousin Shivaun went to work in 9th grade and never graduated because she had no time to study.

2
Reading the Prompt

Topic: SCHOOL ATTENDANCE

When you have a writing assignment in school or when you are asked to write an essay on a test, you are usually given a ***prompt***. The prompt is the question or topic you are being asked to write about. Learning to read and understand the prompt is a key to writing a successful essay.

Here is the prompt for the persuasive essay that you will be working with in Chapters 3-6.

> Your local school district is considering a new attendance policy. This policy states that students who miss more than ten days of class a semester will lose credit for the course.
>
> Write a letter to your local school board, presenting reasons why you agree or disagree with this proposed policy.

Take a moment to think about your immediate responses. Then follow the steps on the next page to help you read the prompt and plan your essay.

Step 1: READ THE PROMPT

How do I feel about this question/situation? What is my position? _____

_____

_____

Step 2: IDENTIFY THE TASK

What am I supposed to do?

- What question/issue am I supposed to address? _____

_____

- What is the purpose of my essay? _____

_____

- Who is my audience? _____

_____

Step 3: READ BETWEEN THE LINES

What other facts might I need to answer this question? _____

_____

Step 4: USE PERSONAL EXPERIENCE

What do I know about this topic?

- Can I tell about an experience of my own? _____
- Can I tell about an experience someone else has had? _____
- Have I read about this topic or seen something about it on TV? _____

Step 5: FORM A FINAL OPINION

How do I feel about this question/issue now? _____

_____

_____

In Chapters 3-6, you will be working with sample essays written in response to this prompt. You will be learning to identify what is missing from each sample and what needs to be changed. Remember that evaluating and revising what someone else has written is one of the best ways to improve your own writing.

3
Revising a Low-Level Essay

Topic: SCHOOL ATTENDANCE

The first essay you will be working with is at the low end of the scoring scale; it would not receive a passing grade. Your job is to read the essay and the analysis of what succeeds in it. Then answer the questions to find out what changes you can make. Finally, follow the directions to revise and improve the essay. (To make the essay easier to read, all spelling errors and most punctuation errors have been removed.)

Remember that a persuasive essay is one in which you take a position and support it with reasons that would convince your audience. In school and on tests, you may be asked to express an opinion on a current issue that has relevance for students, such as the one in the sample prompt you have already read.

Here is that sample prompt again:

> Your local school district is considering a new attendance policy. This policy states that students who miss more than ten days of class a semester will lose credit for the course.
>
> Write a letter to your local school board, presenting reasons why you agree or disagree with this proposed policy.

Here is an example of an essay that would probably receive a low grade. (To make this essay easier to read, all spelling errors and some punctuation errors have been removed.)

> Dear Members of the School Board:
>
> I go to school every day, even when I don't feel well or don't feel like it. I know I have to because you can't get good grades unless you go to school and if you don't finish school you can't get a job. Like my Uncle Lester. So why should someone do whatever he likes and still get good grades? So I think this is a good rule.
>
> Sincerely,

What This Paper Has

This essay probably would not receive a passing grade. Nevertheless, it has some good points that could be made even better. Strengthening these points and fixing some of the weaknesses would greatly improve it and might even turn it into a successful essay.

Read the essay again and notice the following strong points:

1. Statement of writer's position

The writer says, "So I think this is a good rule."

2. Two reasons

The writer says both, ". . . you can't get good grades unless you go to school" and ". . . if you don't finish school you can't get a job."

3. Some support

The writer describes a personal experience: "I go to school every day, even when I don't feel well or don't feel like it." The writer also mentions one example without elaborating it.

4. Some control of language

The sentence structure and punctuation are fairly good. However, there is one long run-on sentence and one fragment. In addition, repeated words make two sentences sound alike. Read the essay aloud and listen for the repetition.

To improve this paper, begin with the strong points and build from there.

Each group of questions below will help you identify what this essay needs. Then you will have a chance to make revisions.

Improving the Essay

▲ The Opening

Answer the following questions:

1. What policy is the school board considering? (The answer is in the prompt.)

_____

2. Does the writer agree with the proposed policy?

_____

3. Where in the essay is the sentence that states the writer's position?

_____

Make the following revision:

Write a new opening that tells what policy is being considered and what the writer's position is.

_____

_____

▲ *Support/Elaboration and Organization*

Here is an outline of one good way to organize the body of a persuasive essay. Compare the sample essay to this outline. What elements shown in the outline does the essay have?

Put a check mark next to each item in the outline that you find in the sample essay.

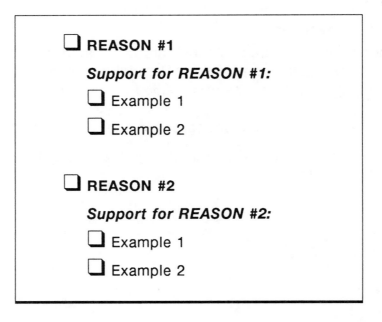

❑ **REASON #1**

Support for REASON #1:

❑ Example 1

❑ Example 2

❑ **REASON #2**

Support for REASON #2:

❑ Example 1

❑ Example 2

Answer the following questions:

1. The first reason the writer gives is "you can't get good grades unless you go to school." What facts or examples can you add to elaborate this reason and make it more convincing?

_____

_____

2. In the second reason, the writer gives Uncle Lester as an example but doesn't tell what happened to him. In one, two, or three sentences, make up a story about Uncle Lester to elaborate this reason. Make sure that the details of your story are connected to finishing school and getting a job, otherwise this story will be a digression.

_____

_____

_____

_____

3. You haven't made any changes yet in the first sentence or the next-to-last sentence. Copy those two sentences here.

_____

_____

Do these sentences go well together? Could you use them to open or close the essay?

_____

_____

Make the following revision:

Rewrite the body of the essay, rearranging sentences and adding facts and examples to elaborate the reasons. Write a separate paragraph for each reason. Follow the outline on the previous page. If you wish, use a separate sheet of paper.

_____

_____

_____

_____

_____

_____

_____

_____

_____

▲ *Language Control*

Answer the following questions:

1. Look again at the original draft of the essay. Identify the run-on sentence by drawing a circle around it.

2. How would you correct it? Write the correct version here.

_____

_____

_____

3. Identify the fragment in the original draft of the essay by underlining it.

4. How would you correct it? Write the corrected sentence here.

_____

_____

_____

Make the following revision:

Read your version of the body of the essay. Do you have any sentence fragments or run-on sentences? Read your sentences aloud. Is there any repetition? If so, rewrite these sentences on your draft.

Finally, proofread your composition and correct any mistakes you find in grammar, punctuation, or spelling.

To Sum Up

This essay has some strong points—but not enough for a passing grade.

Here is a summary of what this paper needed. Check your revision. Did you make all the changes on this list?

1. **A good opening that is a clear statement—**

   —of the proposed policy

   —of the writer's position

2. **Better organization**

   • State writer's position closer to beginning.

   • Avoid digressions and unconnected ideas.

3. **More and better support/elaboration**

   • Use facts and examples to elaborate reasons.

   • Make sure examples contain enough details to be convincing.

4. **Language control**

   • Avoid run-on sentences.

   • Avoid sentence fragments.

   • Avoid repetition.

4
Revising a Middle-Level Essay

Topic: SCHOOL ATTENDANCE

Here is an example of an average or slightly below-average essay, based on the prompt about school attendance that you have been working with. (If you want to review the prompt, you will find it at the beginning of both Chapter 2 and Chapter 3.)

The essay in this chapter needs some work to make sure it will have a passing grade. As you did in the last chapter, read the essay and the analysis of what succeeds in it. Then answer the questions to find out how you can improve the essay, and follow the directions to revise it. You will begin with the strong points and build from there. (Remember that all spelling errors and most punctuation errors have been removed to make the essay easier to read.)

Dear Members of the School Board:

(1)   Why do they have to treat us like children? Why can't we make up our own minds about what we do with our own time? This really makes me mad.

(2)   Besides, suppose you got sick or something. Or suppose you broke a leg. It's not the same thing as cutting classes.

(3)   If I miss classes, I'm already getting punished because I have to make up the work anyway, and I might not get as good grades on my tests because I missed stuff in class, and anyway, some teachers give you zeros for not participating in class, so my grade would get lowered anyway. My grade in English got lowered last year because this kid kept talking to me and passing me notes when I didn't want him to. And if I'm willing to accept those consequences and I can still get a passing grade, why should the system make me lose credit for the course?

(4)   One of the things we're supposed to learn in school is how to be responsible. So we need to make our own decisions, or we'll never learn how.

Sincerely,

What This Paper Has

Read the essay again and notice the following strong points:

1. **Two reasons**

   The writer asks and later answers the question, "why can't we make up our own minds?" The writer also states, ". . . suppose you got sick or something."

2. **Good elaboration of one reason**

   The long third paragraph answers the question, "Why can't we make up our own minds?" by discussing the writer's willingness to accept the consequences of his/her actions. However, the paragraph is spoiled by a story that doesn't belong.

3. **Some sense of organization**

   Each of the two reasons is presented in a separate paragraph. The composition also has an opening and a closing.

4. **Fairly good control of language**

   Sentence length and structure are interesting and varied, although there is one sentence that is too long.

Each group of questions below will help you identify what this essay needs. Then you will have a chance to make revisions.

Improving the Essay

▲ The Opening: Paragraph 1

Answer the following questions:

1. What policy is the school board considering? (The answer is in the prompt.)

   _____

   _____

2. Does the writer agree with the proposed policy? _____

3. How do you know? _____

4. Has the writer clearly stated his/her position in the essay? _____

5. How would you describe the tone of the opening—angry, or calm and logical?

_____

6. Do you think this tone will help persuade the audience—the members of the

school board? _____

Make the following revision:

Rewrite the opening paragraph. Tell what policy is being considered and what the writer's position is. Change the tone to one that will help persuade the audience. (Look at the closing for an example of an appropriate tone.)

_____

_____

_____

▲ Paragraph 2

Answer the following questions:

1. What is the main idea of the second paragraph? _____

_____

2. Is it stated clearly? _____

3. How does the writer develop the main idea? _____

_____

_____

4. The writer gives some details in this paragraph, but not enough. What other facts or examples can you think of that would support the writer's reason? Use ideas or information from your own experience or from what you have read or seen on TV, and jot them down here.

_____

_____

_____

Make the following revision:

Rewrite paragraph 2, stating the main idea clearly. Add some new facts or examples for support. Begin this paragraph with a word or phrase like "first" or "in the first place."

_____

_____

_____

_____

▲ *Paragraph 3*

Answer the following questions:

1. What is the main idea of the third paragraph? _____

_____

_____

2. List the details that support this idea. _____

_____

_____

3. Which sentence does not support the main idea of the paragraph? _____

_____

_____

4. One sentence in this paragraph is especially long and difficult to read. Which sentence is it?

_____

_____

_____

_____

Make the following revision:

Rewrite paragraph 3. Make the sentence that is too long into two or more separate sentences. Take out the sentence that doesn't belong. Begin this paragraph with a transitional word or phrase such as "second," "also," or "in addition."

_____

_____

_____

_____

_____

_____

_____

▲ *Paragraph 4*

Answer the following questions:

1. Is this a good closing? Why or why not? _____

_____

_____

2. What idea in paragraph 1 is the closing related to? _____

_____

_____

Make the following revision:

Add a transitional word or phrase to tell the readers that this is the closing paragraph. Although this paragraph is otherwise complete, you may want to make some additional changes of your own.

_____

_____

_____

_____

_____

_____

▲ *Language Control*

Answer the following questions:

1. Look again at the original draft of the essay. Who does "they" refer to in the first sentence of paragraph 1? What does "something" refer to in the first sentence of paragraph 2? What does "stuff" refer to in the first sentence of paragraph 3? If you don't know, no one else will either. What could you substitute for these vague words?

   _____

   _____

   _____

   _____

2. In a formal essay or letter, it's not a good idea to begin a sentence with "and" or "so." Which sentences begin this way?

   _____

   _____

   _____

Make the following revision:

Read your version of the essay. Do you have any run-ons, sentence fragments, or sentences that are long and difficult to read? Do you use vague words like "they," "stuff," or "something"? Do you use transitional words to introduce each paragraph?

Do you use transitional words to link your supporting ideas (elaboration) to your main reasons?

Finally, remember that good persuasion respects the feeling of the audience. Check your draft for words and sentences that sound angry. Make whatever changes you need on your draft.

As a last step, proofread your essay and correct any mistakes you find in grammar, punctuation, or spelling.

To Sum Up

This essay has a sense of organization and is somewhat elaborated. To make sure of a passing grade, however, the writer needs to develop each reason completely, using examples that are relevant. The writer also needs to persuade his or her readers without sounding angry.

Here is a summary of what this paper needed. Check your revision. Did you make all the changes on the list?

1. **An opening that clearly and calmly states—**

   —the proposed policy

   —the writer's position

2. **Additional support/elaboration**

   - Give a clear statement of each reason.
   - Provide relevant details to develop each reason fully.

3. **Better organization**

   - Avoid digressions.
   - Use transitional words to connect ideas.

4. **Language control**

   - Avoid vague words.
   - Avoid long, confusing sentences.
   - Avoid beginning sentences with "and" or "so."

5. **More awareness of audience**

   - Use appropriate persuasive language

5

Analyzing a Successful Essay

Topic: SCHOOL ATTENDANCE

Here is an example of an above-average essay based on the prompt about school attendance. (Once again, if you want to review the prompt, go to the beginning of either Chapter 2 or Chapter 3.)

Although this essay could be improved, it would certainly receive a passing grade as it is; it is a good response to the prompt. This essay is a good model for you to look at and think about in preparation for writing your own persuasive essay.

Dear Members of the School Board:

(1)   I think the School Board's proposed policy is a good idea. Students shouldn't get credit for a class if they are absent more than 10 times in one semester. When students are absent too much, their school work suffers, and they make things hard for the other students and for the teachers.

(2)   One reason I like this law is that it helps you prepare for the real world. You just can't stay away from work because you don't feel like going. If you stayed away from your job for a week without having a very good reason, you'd probably be fired.

(3)   Even though when you miss school, you can make up the written work and the tests, that's not enough. If you're not in class, you miss discussions and a lot of the teacher's explanations. For example, in science you learn a lot when the teacher answers questions or explains something you didn't understand in the textbook. Also, when you're trying to learn a language, you need to be there to practice speaking and listening.

(4)   It's also hard for the teacher when you just drop into class when you feel like it. If she's teaching something, and you weren't there for the first part of it, she has to try to teach you everything you missed. Then the rest of the class has to wait for you to catch up.

Letter continues on the next page . . .

(5)   Some students are afraid that this new policy will hurt them if they're out sick for a long time. I don't think they have to worry as long as they have a medical excuse. This policy was meant to get rid of the problem of cutting, and I think we need it.

Sincerely,

Analyzing a Successful Essay

This sample can serve as a model for organizing your own essay. In addition, when you analyze the model, you can find out what strategies the writer used to make the essay successful.

▲ *The Opening: Paragraph 1*

- Does the writer give you a clear idea of what the issue is and what the writer's position is?

  _____

- Does the essay have a strong opening? _____

It is clear from the beginning what stand the writer has taken. The writer adds strength to the opening by briefly stating some of the reasons that he/she feels this way. Indicating some of your reasons at the start helps you organize your thoughts and lets your readers know that you will be presenting a logical argument.

▲ *The Body: Paragraphs 2-4*

- Does each paragraph discuss a different reason? _____

- Does the writer give enough details to support each of the reasons? _____

- Do the writer's reasons make sense, and are they appropriate for the audience?

  _____

- Is the writer's tone reasonable and convincing? _____

- Does the writer stick to the topic? _____

- Are transitional words used to show how paragraphs are connected? _____

- Do the word choice and sentence structure help make the composition interesting?

  _____

ELABORATION: *Writing Good Reasons*

Paragraphs 2-4 are the body of the essay. The writer's reasons for supporting the supposed policy are developed in this part of the essay. Notice that the writer chooses reasons that will convince the stated audience.

Although there are three reasons in this essay, a successful essay can also have two reasons that are well developed.

Here are some tips to help you choose convincing reasons.

1. Choose reasons that you are able to support. For example, "cutting classes will ruin your life" is a reason that is difficult to prove. If you choose a reason that you don't know anything about or that is exaggerated and unrealistic, you will not be able to elaborate this part of your essay convincingly. Jotting down ideas beforehand or writing an outline will help you discard reasons you can't support.

2. Keep your audience in mind. Choose reasons that mean something to your audience. To select the reasons that are most appropriate for the position you've taken and for your audience, try asking questions like the following:

   • **Is It Necessary?** Does it need to be done, or do you need it?

   • **Does It Benefit Anyone?** Is it good for you or for someone else?

   • **Is It Important To Your Personal Values?** Does it meet your own sense of what is right or good?

   • **Is It Important For Society?** Is it right or good for most people?

   • **Is The Cost Reasonable?** Is it worth it, not only in dollars but in time, effort, and so on?

3. Remember to support your opinion with facts, examples, and other details. You don't need to avoid opinions; you just need to be able to tell the difference between an opinion and a fact. Avoid supporting an opinion with another opinion.

4. Let your readers know how strongly you feel about the subject, but don't exaggerate your feelings or use abusive language. Remember that persuasion means winning someone over, not beating someone over the head.

ORGANIZATION

In each paragraph of the body of this essay, the writer presents a different reason for the position he/she has taken. The rest of each paragraph contains the details supporting that reason. There are no digressions, and transitional words and phrases help connect the paragraphs.

Here is an outline of a successful essay:

PARAGRAPH 1	Opening

PARAGRAPH 2	Reason #1
	Support for Reason #1
	    Example 1
	    Example 2

PARAGRAPH 3	Reason #2
	Support for Reason #2
	    Example 1
	    Example 2

PARAGRAPH 4	Reason #3
	Support for Reason #3
	    Example 1
	    Example 2

PARAGRAPH 5	Closing

Now go back and look at the successful essay at the beginning of this chapter. Notice how this outline applies to the essay. It is the structure of what the student has written.

Compare each paragraph of the essay with the outline. Take each item in the outline, one at a time, and find the sentence in the essay that corresponds to it.

If you can remember this outline and follow it in your own writing, you will write a successful persuasive essay.

LANGUAGE CONTROL

The structure of the sentences and the writer's choice of words is interesting and varied. The grammar, spelling, and punctuation are also correct.

▲ *The Closing: Paragraph 5*

- Does the composition have a strong closing? _____

To conclude the essay, this writer anticipates an argument for the opposite position and answers it. This is an effective technique to use in a persuasive essay because it deals with a question your readers might have. The last sentence ends the essay with a strong restatement of the writer's position.

6

Writing and Evaluating Your Own Essay

Topic: USING SCHOOL MONEY

You are going to write an essay of your own, using a new prompt.

> Your school has received a large sum of money that must be used next year. The school board has discussed how to spend the money and has narrowed its choices to the following two:
>
> - Enough word processors so that all students can write their papers on computers, or—
>
> - New uniforms for the football team and the marching band and new instruments for the band.
>
> How do you think the money should be spent? Write a letter to the school board, stating your position and the reasons for it.

Reading the Prompt

Follow the steps below to help you read the prompt and plan your essay.

Step 1: READ THE PROMPT

How do I feel about this question/situation? What is my position? _____

_____

_____

Steps continue on the next page . . .

Step 2: IDENTIFY THE TASK

What am I supposed to do?

• What question/issue am I supposed to address? _____

_____

• What is the purpose of my essay? _____

_____

• Who is my audience? _____

_____

Step 3: READ BETWEEN THE LINES

What other facts might I need to answer this question? _____

_____

Step 4: USE PERSONAL EXPERIENCE

What do I know about this topic?

• Can I tell about an experience of my own? _____

• Can I tell about an experience someone else has had? _____

• Have I read about this topic or seen something about it on TV? _____

Step 5: FORM A FINAL OPINION

How do I feel about this question/issue now? _____

_____

_____

Mapping the Essay

When you have finished the last step of Reading the Prompt, you will have decided what your position is. You will also have begun to think about how to support your position. Complete the steps below to finish planning your essay.

1. List as many reasons as you think of that support the position you have taken. You can write just words or phrases instead of sentences.

    _____

    _____

    _____

    _____

2. Now evaluate your reasons. Are they sensible ones? Will they appeal to your audience? Can they be supported easily? Circle each reason that you think will really persuade your readers.

3. Rewrite every reason you circled above, turning it into the topic sentence of a paragraph. Beneath each topic sentence, jot down two or three facts or details that support the reason. (These do not have to be sentences.)

    Reason #1: _____

    _____

    Supporting facts and details: _____

    _____

    Reason #2: _____

    _____

    Supporting facts and details: _____

    _____

    Reason #3: _____

    _____

    Supporting facts and details: _____

    _____

4. Write some transitional words or phrases that you might use to show the connections between paragraphs.

   Between Paragraph 1 and Paragraph 2: _____

   _____

   Between Paragraph 1 and Paragraph 3: _____

   _____

5. For your opening, state the issue and your position. _____

   _____

   _____

   Jot down any reasons that you can mention briefly in an opening. _____

   _____

   _____

6. If you have any special ideas about the closing of your essay, jot them down here. Remember that one possibility is to answer an argument from the other side of the issue. For an example, look at the last paragraph of the successful essay in the last chapter.

   _____

   _____

   _____

   _____

   _____

Writing the First Draft

Use what you have written in these mapping activities to write a first draft of your essay. Write your draft on a separate sheet of paper.

Evaluating and Improving the Essay

When you have finished your draft, read what you have written. Then use the following form to analyze your essay. Check the appropriate boxes, and jot down any comments you wish. You can work on your own or with a partner.

1. Does the essay give you a clear idea of what the issue is and what the writer's position is?

   ☐ yes ☐ no   Comments: _____

2. Does the essay have a strong opening? For example, does the opening briefly mention the reasons that will support the writer's position?

   ☐ yes ☐ no   Comments: _____

3. Does each paragraph discuss a different reason?

   ☐ yes ☐ no   Comments: _____

4. Does the writer give enough details to support each of the reasons?

   ☐ yes ☐ no   Comments: _____

5. Do the writer's reasons make sense, and are they appropriate for the audience?

   ☐ yes ☐ no   Comments: _____

6. Is the writer's tone reasonable and convincing?

   ☐ yes ☐ no   Comments: _____

7. Does the writer stick to the topic?

   ☐ yes ☐ no   Comments: _____

8. Are transitional words used to show how paragraphs are connected?

   ☐ yes ☐ no   Comments: _____

9. Do the word choice and sentence structure make the essay interesting?

   ☐ yes ☐ no   Comments: _____

10. Does the essay have a strong closing? For example, does it restate the writer's position clearly and forcefully? Or answer an argument from the other side?

    ☐ yes ☐ no   Comments: _____

Decide what changes would improve your essay, and make these changes on your paper. Remember that these sorts of improvements can make a difference in your grade.

For extra practice, make a final copy of your revised essay. This time, make sure that the grammar, punctuation, and spelling are all correct.

7

Reading the Prompt

Topic: A MOTORCYCLE HELMET LAW

You have completed one full set of practice and mastery activities—reading a prompt, revising two essays, examining a successful essay, and mapping and writing your own essay.

The two prompts you worked with asked you to take a position on a school-related issue. Now you are going to complete an additional set of practice and mastery activities. This time, the prompt asks you to take a position on an issue that affects the community at large. You will begin as you did before, by making sure that you understand the prompt.

> As a result of many serious motorcycle accidents, your state's lawmakers are considering a law that says that all motorcycle riders have to wear protective helmets. What is your position concerning such a law?
>
> Write a letter to the editor of your local newspaper stating your position and supporting it with convincing reasons.

Follow the steps below to help you read this prompt and plan your essay.

Step 1: READ THE PROMPT

How do I feel about this question/situation? What is my position? _____

_____

_____

Step 2: IDENTIFY THE TASK

What am I supposed to do?

• What question/issue am I supposed to address? _____

_____

• What is the purpose of my essay? _____

_____

- Who is my audience? _____

_____

Step 3: READ BETWEEN THE LINES

What other facts might I need to answer this question? _____

_____

Step 4: USE PERSONAL EXPERIENCE

What do I know about this topic?

- Can I tell about an experience of my own? _____

- Can I tell about an experience someone else has had? _____

- Have I read about this topic or seen something about it on TV? _____

Step 5: FORM A FINAL OPINION

How do I feel about this question/issue now? _____

_____

_____

In the next few chapters you will be working with sample essays written in response to this prompt. As you did before, you will learn to identify what is missing from each sample and what needs to be changed. Remember that evaluating and revising what someone else has written is one of the best ways to improve your own writing.

8
Revising a Low-Level Essay

Topic: A MOTORCYCLE HELMET LAW

The first essay in this set of practice activities is at the low end of the scoring scale. Like the low-level essay in Chapter 3, it probably would not receive a passing grade.

Read the essay and the analysis of what succeeds in it. Then answer the questions to find out what changes you can make. Finally, follow the directions to revise and improve the essay. (As usual, to make the essay easier to read, all spelling errors and some punctuation errors have been removed.)

Remember that this essay has been written in response to the prompt at the beginning of Chapter 7.

Dear Editor:

It's dangerous to ride a motorcycle. Without a helmet. I know about a guy who did that, my friend told me about him, and he got hurt. It wasn't even his fault. He was going to see his girlfriend. She lives in Cranetown. So I think this is a good law. He had his whole life to live. And now it's wasted.

Sincerely,

What This Paper Has

Read the essay again and notice the following strong points:

1. **Statement of writer's position**

   The writer says, "So I think this is a good law."

2. **One reason**

   The writer opens with, "It's dangerous to ride a motorcycle."

3. **Some support**

   The writer uses a personal anecdote as an example: "I know about a guy . . . and he got hurt. . . . He had his whole life to live. And now it's wasted."

4. **Some control of language**

   Although there is one fragment and one long, awkward run-on sentence, the rest of the sentences are correct. They are, however, monotonous. Read the essay aloud and listen to how much the sentences sound alike.

Often, the first draft you write looks like a low-level paper. You have some good ideas, but they may be out of order or not completely developed. How do you improve this paper—maybe turn it into a paper that will receive a passing grade? Begin with the strong points you already have and build from there.

Practice with the essay you just finished reading. Each group of questions below will help you identify what the essay needs. Then you will have a chance to make revisions.

Improving the Essay

▲ The Opening

Answer the following questions:

1. What law are the lawmakers considering? (Look at the prompt to answer this question).

   _____

   _____

2. What is the writer's position with regard to this law?

   _____

   _____

3. Where in the essay is the sentence that states the writer's position?

   _____

   _____

Make the following revision:

Write a new opening that tells what law is being considered and what the writer's position is.

_____

_____

_____

_____

_____

_____

▲ *Support/Elaboration and Organization*

Answer the following questions:

1. This writer gives one reason for taking this position. What is that reason? (Write your answer in a full sentence.)

   _____

   _____

2. As an example to support this position, the writer tells a story. Sum up the story in one sentence.

   _____

   _____

3. Look again at the story the writer tells. Two sentences don't belong because they bring in information that doesn't support the writer's reason. Which two sentences are they?

   _____

   _____

4. Although the example the writer gives is a good one, it is not enough. What other facts or examples can you think of that would support the writer's reason? Use ideas or information from your own experience or from what you have read or seen on TV, and jot them down here.

   _____

   _____

5. Choose one idea that you can develop into at least two sentences. Make sure it supports the writer's reason. Write your sentences here.

   _____

   _____

   _____

Make the following revision:

Rewrite the body of the essay, taking out the sentences that don't belong and adding the facts or example you just developed.

_____

_____

_____

_____

_____

▲ *Language Control*

Answer the following questions:

1. Look again at the original draft of the essay. Identify the sentence fragment.

    _____

    _____

2. How would you correct it? Write the corrected sentence here.

    _____

    _____

3. One sentence is especially awkward and difficult to read. Identify it.

    _____

    _____

4. How could you improve it? Write your version here.

    _____

    _____

    _____

    _____

    _____

Make the following revision:

Read your revision of the body of the essay. Do you have any sentence fragments or sentences that are awkward and difficult to read? Do you have too many sentences that sound alike? If so, rewrite them on your draft.

_____

_____

_____

_____

_____

_____

To Sum Up

This writer has made a good beginning, but it is only a beginning. It is not enough for a passing grade.

Here is a summary of what this paper needed. Check your revision. Did you make all the changes on this list?

1. **A good opening that is a clear statement—**

    —of the proposed law.

    —of the writer's position.

2. **More and better support/elaboration**

    • Make sure examples are strong enough to provide support.

    • Use facts to support your feelings.

3. **Better organization**

    • State writer's position closer to beginning.

    • Avoid digression/unconnected ideas.

4. **Language control**

    • Avoid sentence fragments.

    • Avoid sentences that are too long and awkward.

    • Avoid sentences that are too short and monotonous.

9
Revising a Middle-Level Essay

Topic: A MOTORCYCLE HELMET LAW

This chapter is based on a second essay on the proposed motorcycle helmet law—this time, an essay that is average or slightly below average. (If you want to review the prompt, it's at the beginning of Chapter 7.) This essay needs improvement in order to be sure of making a passing grade.

Follow the procedure you did before. First, read the essay and the analysis of what succeeds in it. Then answer the questions to find out how you can improve it. Last of all, follow the directions for revision, building on the essay's strong points. (Again, all spelling errors and most punctuation errors have been removed to make the essay easier to read.)

Dear Editor:

(1)   I don't like the idea of a law like wearing a helmet when you ride on a motorcycle that tells me I have to do something when I should be the one who decides.

(2)   A helmet doesn't protect you from everything. You could still hurt your back. That could be as bad as hurting your head you could be paralyzed for life. How would you like to be completely helpless? Do you think anyone would take care of you?

(3)   This is a free country. They shouldn't try to stop you from doing certain things even if they are dangerous. My friend Jim has been smoking for five years. He's got a real bad cough and he knows it would go away if he stopped smoking, but he's not going to give it up. Why should he?

(4)   My last reason is that if you do something that only hurts you, why should a law tell you not to. Why don't they worry about getting rid of drug dealers and murderers instead?

Sincerely,

What This Paper Has

Read the essay again and notice the following strong points.

1. **Statement of writer's position**

   The writer says, "I don't like the idea of a law like wearing a helmet when you ride on a motorcycle."

2. **Two reasons**

   The writer states, "A helmet doesn't protect you from everything" and "They shouldn't try to stop you from doing certain things even if they are dangerous."

3. **Some elaboration of the reasons**

   The writer uses an example—"You could even be wearing a helmet and still hurt your back"—and a personal anecdote—"My friend Jim has been smoking for five years."

4. **Some sense of organization**

   Paragraphs 2 and 3 both contain a reason and the details supporting that reason.

5. **Fairly good control of language**

   The writer's language is generally clear and the sentences are varied; the ideas flow smoothly from one to another.

This paper contains some good ideas, but it might not receive a passing grade because it also contains one of the most common and most serious student errors. The writer indicates that there are three reasons, but there are actually only two. The "reasons" in paragraphs 3 and 4 are really the same reason, However, the author gives this reason twice, as though it were two separate reasons.

This is a difficult fault to spot unless you are looking for it Go back and read paragraphs 3 and 4 again, and notice how the two "reasons" are really the same.

In addition, the writer makes another common error. The tone of the essay—sometimes aggressive and sometimes complaining—is inappropriate for a formal persuasive essay.

Use this essay to practice turning a shaky paper into one that will definitely pass. Each group of questions below will help you identify what the essay needs. Then you will have a chance to make revisions.

Improving the Essay

▲ *The Opening*

Answer the following questions:

1. What law are your state's lawmakers considering? (Look at the prompt to answer this question.)

   _____

   _____

2. What reasons does the writer give for objecting to this law? (Answer in your own words.)

   _____

   _____

3. Which word would you use to describe the tone of the first sentence in the essay— angry, humorous, or logical?

   _____

Make the following revision:

Rewrite the opening. Tell what law is being considered and the reasons the writer objects to it. Present your ideas in a logical way.

   _____

   _____

   _____

▲ *Paragraph 2*

Answer the following questions:

1. What is the main idea of the second paragraph?

   _____

   _____

2. List the details that support this idea.

   _____

   _____

3. Which two sentences do not support the main idea of this paragraph?

_____

_____

4. This is the part of the essay where you need to inform your audience by presenting facts and examples. Are there enough details in this paragraph to support the main idea?

_____

_____

5. What kinds of facts or examples could be added to this paragraph? Jot some down here.

_____

_____

Make the following revision:

Rewrite paragraph 2, taking out the sentences that don't belong and adding some new facts or examples. Remember that if you sound angry, you will probably make your audience angry. To win people over, you need to respect their feelings as well as to express your own.

_____

_____

_____

_____

▲ *Paragraph 3*

Answer the following questions:

1. What is the main idea of the third paragraph?

_____

_____

2. Is it stated clearly?

_____

3. The writer gives an example that needs to be developed further. The connection between the main idea of the paragraph and the example needs to be stated. Write a sentence that would make this connection.

_____

_____

4. This paragraph could be improved even more with some additional examples. What kinds of examples could be added? Jot some down here.

_____

_____

Make the following revision:

Rewrite paragraph 3, stating the main idea clearly. Add one or more examples, and state the connection between each example and the main idea of the paragraph. Remember, too, that your job is to win over your audience.

_____

_____

_____

_____

_____

▲ Paragraph 4

Answer the following questions:

1. Does the last paragraph really contain a new reason, or does it repeat a reason that the writer has already given?

_____

_____

2. Can you think of an additional reason to support the writer's position? If so, make a note of it here.

_____

_____

3. Does the last sentence make a good ending? Why or why not?

_____

_____

Make the following revision:

There are two ways to revise this paragraph:

• If you can think of another reason, write a new paragraph. Make sure that you develop the reason well with facts or an example.

• Or you can turn this paragraph into a closing statement that sums up the writer's position.

_____

_____

_____

_____

▲ Language Control

Answer the following questions:

1. Look again at the original draft of the essay. One sentence is especially long and difficult to read. Identify it.

_____

_____

2. How could you improve it? Write your version here.

_____

_____

3. Find the run-on sentence in paragraph 2. How would you correct it? Write your correction here.

_____

_____

4. Who does "they" refer to in the second sentence of paragraph 3 and the last sentence of the essay? If you don't know, no one else will either. What could you substitute for "they" in each of these sentences?

_____

_____

_____

_____

5. What transitional words can you add at the beginning of paragraph 2 and the beginning of paragraph 3 to help the reader understand how the paragraphs are connected?

_____

_____

_____

_____

6. Do you like the tone of the last sentence in the essay? Do you think it belongs in a formal, persuasive letter?

_____

Make the following revision:

Read your revision of the essay. Do you have any run-ons or sentences that are too long and difficult to read? Do you have any vague words like "they"? Do you have any sentences that might offend your readers or make them angry? If so, re-write them on your draft. Add any transitions that are needed.

To Sum Up

This paper might get a passing grade. To be sure of passing, the writer needs to make sure that each reason given is really a separate reason and that the tone is persuasive, not angry and argumentative. The writer also needs to express ideas more clearly and show the connections between them.

Here is a summary of what this paper needed. Check your revision. Did you make all the changes on the list?

1. **More awareness of audience**
   - Use appropriate language.

2. **Better organization**
   - Avoid digression—that is, switching to another subject.
   - Use transitions.

3. **Additional support/elaboration**
   - Use relevant examples.
   - Avoid "hidden repetition"—saying the same thing in two different ways.
   - Details should be there for a reason, not just put in as unconnected items.

4. **Language control**
   - Avoid sentences that are too long and hard to read.
   - Avoid run-on sentences.
   - Avoid the use of vague "they."

10

Analyzing a Successful Essay

Topic: A MOTORCYCLE HELMET LAW

Here is an example of an above-average essay on the subject of the proposed motorcycle helmet law. This essay would definitely receive a passing grade. Although it could be improved, it succeeds in responding to the prompt. (If you want to review the prompt, it's at the beginning of Chapter 7.)

This essay is a good model for you to analyze in preparation for writing your own persuasive essay. By identifying both what the essay's strong points are and how it could be improved, you will increase your chances of writing a successful essay yourself.

Dear Editor,

(1)   Our state is considering a law about wearing a helmet when you ride a motorcycle. I am writing because I think that this would be a good law. We need this law because it is the only way to prevent serious head injuries. And preventing these injuries is very important.

(2)   A head injury can be a kind of living death. I saw a report on TV about what happens to accident victims who have head injuries. More than half of them go into a coma that can last anywhere from a few days to a few months. Some can even last for years. The person stays in a hospital or a nursing home tied up to a machine that helps them breathe. Keeping somebody alive like this costs a lot of money—especially if the coma lasts a long time.

(3)   Also, a head injury isn't something you get over quickly. Even after you get out of the coma, it could affect you for the rest of your life. My cousin Tina was twelve years old when she fell out of the cottonwood tree right onto a big rock. She got a broken arm and a fractured skull. Her arm got completely better but her brain didn't. She's had really bad headaches ever since. She can't even hold down a regular job because she never knows when she'll be okay.

(4)   I hope you'll think about what I said.

Sincerely,

What This Paper Has

Read the essay again and notice the following strong points.

1. **Awareness of audience**

   The writer uses an objective tone throughout.

2. **Clear statement of the problem and of the writer's position**

   The writer opens with, "Our state is considering a law about wearing a helmet when you ride a motorcycle. I am writing because I think that this would be a good law."

3. **Two reasons**

   The writer begins paragraph 2 by stating, "A head injury can be a kind of living death," and opens paragraph 3 by stating, "Also, a head injury isn't something you get over quickly."

4. **Elaboration of reasons with relevant facts and examples**

   The writer includes facts from a television program—"I saw a report on TV . . . especially if the coma lasts a long time"—and uses a personal anecdote as an example—"My cousin Tina . . . she never knows when she'll be okay."

5. **Good sense of organization**

   Paragraphs 2 and 3 both begin with a reason and include the details supporting that reason.

6. **Strong beginning**

   The writer begins with a clear statement of the problem and of his/her position. The writer makes a strong statement about why he or she has taken this position.

7. **Clear language; varied sentence structure**

   The writer varies the sentence openings and uses lively language, as in these examples: "Keeping somebody alive like this costs a lot of money—especially if the coma lasts a long time" and "Even after you get out of the coma, it could affect you for the rest of your life."

Writing an essay like this one means that you know how to express yourself clearly and how to get a point across to an audience. You are a competent, dependable writer and should do well in writing assignments in school and on the job.

You may also have the ability to do even better. What are some of the ways the paper on page 63 could be improved?

Improving the Essay

▲ Persuasive Language

The words and phrases you use should let your reader know how strongly you feel about the subject. Don't exaggerate your feelings, and remember that persuasion means winning someone over, not beating someone over the head.

For example, the opening sentences of the essay could be rewritten this way:

> Our state is considering an important new law about wearing a helmet when you ride a motorcycle. I am writing because I feel very strongly that this law should be passed. We need this law . . .

▲ Persuasive Techniques

It's always a good idea to anticipate and answer, or rebut, at least one argument that the other side might use. In this case, an opponent of the law might point out that helmets don't prevent other kinds of serious injuries. This point could be rebutted by adding a paragraph following paragaph 3. Here's an example:

> Opponents of this law have pointed out that helmets don't prevent other kinds of serious injuries—for example, broken bones or spinal injuries. That is true. However, it seems a shame not to prevent the injuries we can prevent. Why increase someone's chances of being seriously injured if we don't have to?

▲ Transitions

These words and phrases are the writer's way of indicating to the reader how ideas are connected to each other. They make the organization of the paper clearer. This paper could use two transitions:

Paragraph 2: *In the first place,* a head injury can . . .

Paragraph 3: *For example,* my cousin Tina . . .

Here are a few other transitional words and phrases that you might find helpful in writing persuasive essays:

for instance	finally	in addition
therefore	furthermore	however
most important	although	equally important
on the other hand	in fact	for these reasons
next	as you can see	

▲ *A Strong Closing*

Writing a good closing is not easy. Often, the best way to close is to make a strong final point. In this case, a rebuttal paragraph like the one shown above would be a good choice.

Another way to close is to use a call to action—a few sentences that ask the reader to do something. For example:

> The law under consideration can keep people from being disabled. Let's do everything we can to get this law passed. I urge everyone to write to their representatives today and ask them to vote for this law.

In any case, if you have a strong closing paragraph, don't weaken it with a sentence like "I hope you'll think about what I said."

To Sum Up

This paper will definitely pass. The writing is clear and well organized, and the reasons make sense and are supported with relevant facts and examples. To get a higher grade, this paper needs a strong closing and more conscious use of persuasive techniques to convince the audience.

Here is a summary of what this paper needed:

1. **More use of persuasive language.**

2. **Use of persuasive techniques to convince the reader.**

3. **More transitions.**

4. **A strong closing.**

11
Writing and Evaluating Your Own Essay

Topic: GUN CONTROL

You are going to write another essay of your own, using a new prompt.

> In response to an increase in gun violence, supporters of gun control laws are urging the federal government to pass a new law requiring the registration of all guns and rifles. Every gun owner would also have to undergo a background check and wait two weeks before receiving a license.
>
> What is your position regarding such a law? Write a letter to your Congressional representative stating your position and supporting it with convincing reasons.

Reading the Prompt

Follow the steps below and on the next page to help you read the prompt and plan your essay.

Step 1: READ THE PROMPT

How do I feel about this question/situation? What is my position? _____

_____

_____

Step 2: IDENTIFY THE TASK

What am I supposed to do?

• What question/issue am I supposed to address? _____

_____

• What is the purpose of my essay? _____

_____

• Who is my audience? _____

_____

Step 3: READ BETWEEN THE LINES

What other facts might I need to answer this question? _____

_____

Step 4: USE PERSONAL EXPERIENCE

What do I know about this topic?

• Can I tell about an experience of my own? _____

• Can I tell about an experience someone else has had? _____

• Have I read about this topic or seen something about it on TV? _____

Step 5: FORM A FINAL OPINION

How do I feel about this question/issue now? _____

_____

_____

Mapping the Essay

Now that you know what you think, your job is to find the best way to persuade someone else that your opinion is a good one. You can do this in two steps.

▲ State Your Opinion Clearly

1. Use precise language.

• Make sure your audience can tell what the original question or issue was.

• Make sure your audience can tell how you feel about this question or issue.

2. Organize your ideas in a way that makes sense.

▲ *State Your Opinion Convincingly*

1. Give reasons for feeling the way you do. Use some of the personal experiences you came up with in *Step 4* of **Reading the Prompt.**

   - Give some facts.

   - Give some examples.

   - Tell a relevant story.

2. State what is wrong with or weak about the other side of the argument

   - Is it practical?

   - Is it realistic?

   - Does it benefit anyone?

3. Use persuasive language

   - Show how important you feel the question or issue is.

   - Urge your audience to share your opinion.

   - Avoid offensive language.

Writing the First Draft

Now write your essay on a separate sheet of paper. Use the steps in the mapping activity as a guide.

Evaluating and Improving the Essay

When you have finished writing, read your draft. Then use the following questions to analyze and improve your essay. You can work on your own or with a partner.

1. Does the writer give you a clear idea of what problem he or she is taking a position on?

   ❑ yes ❑ no   Comments: _____

2. Is the writer's position clear?

   ❑ yes ❑ no   Comments: _____

3. Does the writer give good reasons for taking this position? If there is more than one reason, are they really different from each other?

   ❑ yes ❑ no   Comments: _____

4. Are the reasons supported by relevant facts and examples?

   ❑ yes ❑ no   Comments: _____

5. Are the reasons elaborated? That is, does the writer provide enough details to make the reasons convincing?

   ❑ yes ❑ no   Comments: _____

6. Is the essay well organized? Can you follow the writer's thoughts? Are there any sentences that don't belong? Has the writer connected ideas and made transitions from one group of thoughts to another?

   ❑ yes ❑ no   Comments: _____

7. Does the essay have a strong opening or a strong closing?

   ❑ yes ❑ no   Comments: _____

8. Does the writer seem to respect the feelings of the audience? Does the writer use an appropriate tone?

   ❑ yes ❑ no   Comments: _____

9. Does the writer use clear language? Has the writer avoided sentences that are too long or difficult to understand? Has the writer varied the sentence structure? Has the writer avoided fragments and run-ons?

   ❑ yes ❑ no   Comments: _____

Decide what works and what can be improved in your essay. Then make the appropriate changes on your paper.

For extra practice, make a final copy of your revised essay. This time, make sure that the grammar, punctuation, and spelling are all correct.

UNIT TWO

WRITING ABOUT ADVANTAGES AND DISADVANTAGES

In the first unit of this book, you worked with persuasive essays. In this type of essay, your purpose is to state your opinion on some topic and to persuade your reader of the correctness of that opinion.

There are other kinds of essays in which you express opinions, but your main purpose is not to persuade or convince your audience. For example, you may be asked to explain the advantages and disadvantages of something. In this kind of essay, your job is to examine both sides of a question. You express your opinion on what you think the good points and bad points are. But you don't make a recommendation or take a position.

This kind of writing is fairly common in everyday life. For example, newspapers and magazines sometimes contain product comparisons that discuss the good points and bad points of each product. The article doesn't come out and say which product is "best," however. It is up to the reader to make the decision on which product is best for his or her needs and wants.

In Unit Two of this book, you will learn how to write this kind of essay.

12

Reading the Prompt

Topic: A SCHOOL DRESS CODE

Here is a prompt that asks you to write an essay that examines advantages and disadvantages. Notice that the prompt asks you to discuss <u>both</u> the good things and the bad things, not just one or the other.

> Many schools are thinking of creating a dress code to make sure that all students come to school dressed appropriately.
>
> There are both good and bad things about having a dress code. Write an essay for your teacher in which you explain both what is good and what is bad about a dress code. Be sure to explain each point fully.

Take a moment to think about your immediate responses. Follow the steps below to help you read this prompt. These steps will give you a head start on planning and organizing your essay.

Step 1: READ THE PROMPT

What advantages and disadvantages come immediately to mind? _____

_____

_____

Step 2: IDENTIFY THE TASK

What am I supposed to do?

• What topic do I have to write about? _____

_____

• What is the purpose of my essay? _____

_____

• Who is my audience? _____

_____

Step 3: READ BETWEEN THE LINES

What other facts might I need to answer this question? _____

_____

Step 4: USE PERSONAL EXPERIENCE

What do I know about this topic?

• What are some of the good things I know about it? _____

_____

• What are some of the bad things I know about it? _____

_____

• Have I read about this topic or seen something about it on TV? _____

Step 5: FORM A FINAL OPINION

Do I want to add any new points? If so, what? _____

_____

Do I want to take out any of the points I first thought of? If so, which ones? _____

_____

_____

In the next three chapters of this section, you will be working with essays written in answer to this prompt, just as you did in Unit One.

13

Revising a Low-Level Essay

Topic: A SCHOOL DRESS CODE

You will begin by working with an essay that would not receive a passing grade. Read the essay and the analysis of what succeeds in it. Then answer the questions to find out what changes you can make. As the last step, follow the directions to revise and improve the essay. (As usual, to make the essay easier to read, all spelling errors and most of the punctuation errors have been removed.)

Here again is the prompt.

> Many schools are thinking of creating a dress code to make sure that all students come to school dressed appropriately.
>
> There are both good and bad things about having a dress code. Write an essay for your teacher in which you explain both what is good and what is bad about a dress code. Be sure to explain each point fully.

Here is the example of an essay that would probably receive a low grade.

> I think it's a good idea to have a dress code because kids might wear the wrong things to school. Like T-shirts that advertise beer. I also think it's a bad idea to have a dress code because we are old enough we should know what to wear. So there are good things and bad things on both sides.

What This Paper Has

This essay would not receive a passing grade. Can you tell why? Look back at the introductory chapter on "How Are Essays Graded?" to see what readers consider important.

Even though this essay would not pass, it has some good points. Read it again and notice the following things:

1. **The topic of the composition is stated clearly.**

   The composition is about a school dress code. The writer is going to examine advantages and disadvantages.

2. **The writer mentions one advantage and develops it slightly by giving an example.**

   "kids might wear the wrong things to school . . . T-shirts that advertise beer."

3. **The writer mentions one disadvantage.**

   "It's a bad idea to have a dress code because we are old enough . . ."

4. **The writer shows how ideas are connected.**

   The writer uses the words "because," "also," and "so."

5. **The writer shows some control of language.**

   Some of the sentences are clear and complete.

To improve this paper, begin with the strong points and build from there. Making the good points even better and fixing some of the weaknesses should earn this composition a higher score.

Although you didn't write this essay, it is your job to revise it. You can use your own ideas and your own examples. Each group of questions below will help you identify what this essay needs. Then you will have a chance to make revisions.

Improving the Essay

▲ Elaboration and Organization

Answer the following questions:

1. The writer gives one reason for saying that a dress code is a good idea and supports it with one example. What other example would help make this reason convincing?

   _____

   _____

2. The reason the writer gives for saying that a dress code is a bad idea is very unclear. Can you rewrite it so that it makes better sense? If so, write your new sentence here.

   _____

   _____

   What other reason can you give?

   _____

   What examples would help make this reason convincing?

   _____

Make the following revision:

Rewrite the essay in two paragraphs, adding the reasons and examples you listed above. Make sure they are clearly stated. Use the chart on page 77 to help you organize your essay.

_____

_____

_____

_____

_____

_____

Paragraph 1

State the topic

Discuss the advantages of the idea

- Give at least one reason.

- Support the reason with an example.

Paragraph 2

Discuss the disadvantages of the idea

- Give at least one reason.

- Support each reason with an example.

▲ *Language Control*

Answer the following questions:

1. Look again at the original draft of the essay. Draw a circle around the sentence fragment. How would you correct it? Write the correct version here.

   _____

   _____

2. Underline the run-on sentence in the original draft. How would you correct it? Write your version here.

   _____

   _____

Make the following revision:

Read your draft of the essay. Do you have any sentence fragments or run-on sentences? If so, rewrite these sentences on your draft.

Finally, proofread your essay and correct any mistakes you find in grammar, punctuation, or spelling.

14

Revising a Middle-Level Essay

Topic: A SCHOOL DRESS CODE

This essay on the topic of a school dress code is slightly below average. In order to have a passing grade, the essay needs to be revised. (If you want to review the prompt, it's at the beginning of Chapters 12 and 13).

First, read the essay and the analysis of what succeeds in it. Find out how to improve it by answering the questions that follow. Then revise the essay, beginning with its strong points and building from there. (Remember that spelling errors and most punctuation errors have been removed.)

(1)   There are good points and bad points in having a dress code. You have to look at both sides. Probably the worst thing is that you have to dress in what someone tells you to dress in. You want to wear a hat you can't. Also haircuts. My friend had the sides of his head shaved and the hair standing up on top.

(2)   But maybe a dress code might be a good thing because kids should look nice when they go to school. But I still really think a dress code is a bad thing. What if it's hot and they say you can't wear shorts. You wouldn't be able to think because your brain would be melting.

(3)   So those are the two sides to having a dress code. That's why it could be either good or bad to have a dress code.

What This Paper Has

Most readers whould give this paper a better grade than the essay in the previous chapter. Do you agree? In what ways is it better?

Read the essay again and notice the following strong points.

1. The topic of the essay is stated clearly.

"There are good points and bad points in having a dress code."

2. **The writer mentions several bad points and develops them by giving examples.**

   The writer uses hats, haircuts, and shorts as examples.

3. **The writer mentions one good point.**

   ". . . kids should look nice when they go to school."

4. **The writer shows how ideas are connected by using the words "also," "but," and "so."**

5. **The writer shows some control of language.**

   Most of the sentences are clear and complete.

Elaboration is the main reason that this essay received a higher grade. Making these good points even better and fixing some of the weaknesses might earn this essay a higher grade.

Each group of questions below will help you identify what this essay needs. Then you will have a chance to make revisions.

Improving the Essay

▲ *Elaboration and Organization*

Answer the following questions:

1. The writer begins the second paragraph by mentioning one good point about having a dress code. What is the rest of this paragraph about?

   _____

   _____

   It is important to keep all the information about bad points together and all the information about good points together. To do this, use the first sentence of paragraph 2 to begin a new paragraph about the good points of a dress code.

2. What does the word "nice" mean in the first sentence of your new paragraph? To make the meaning clear, add some examples that tell what "nice" clothes are. For instance, you might say that nice clothes are the kind you wear to a family party.

   _____

   _____

3. What are some reasons for wearing nice clothes? How do other people treat you when you wear nice clothes? How do you feel? List some reasons here.

   _____

   _____

4. A good example can make your reasons more convincing. Think of something that has happened to you or someone you know that shows how important it can be to dress nicely.

   _____

   _____

Make the following revision:

On a separate sheet of paper, rewrite the composition, adding the reasons and examples you listed above to develop your new paragraph about good points. Use the following plan to organize your essay.

Paragraph 1

   State the topic

   Discuss one or more of the bad points

   - give at least one reason

   - support each reason with an example

Paragraph 2

   Discuss the rest of the bad points

   - give at least one reason

   - support each reason with an example

Paragraph 3

   Discuss one or more good points

   - give at least one reason for each

   - support at least one reason with an example

▲ *Language Control*

Answer the following questions:

1. Look again at the original draft of the essay. Read the fourth sentence in paragraph 1 aloud ("You want to wear a hat you can't"). Does it sound right to you? What changes can you make so that it will sound right? (There is more than one way to make this sentence clearer.)

    _____

    _____

2. Draw a circle around the sentence fragment in paragraph 1. How would you correct it? Write your version here.

    _____

    _____

3. Sentences 5 and 6 of paragraph 1 provide an example that supports one of the bad points of a dress code. However, something is missing. You need to tell your readers that this is an example, and you need to tell them what can happen to someone who doesn't follow the school dress code. What are some ways that you can make these changes?

    _____

    _____

    _____

    _____

Make the following revision:

Read your draft of the essay. Do you have any unclear sentences or sentence fragments? If so, rewrite these sentences on your draft.

Finally, proofread your essay and correct any mistakes you find in grammar, punctuation, or spelling.

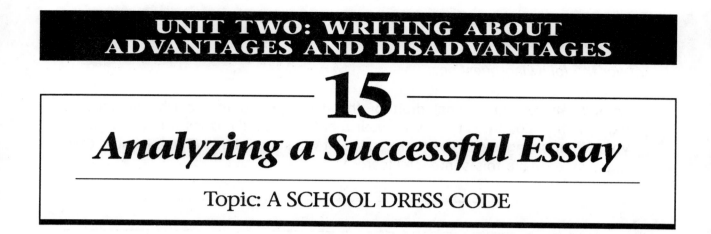

UNIT TWO: WRITING ABOUT ADVANTAGES AND DISADVANTAGES

15

Analyzing a Successful Essay

Topic: A SCHOOL DRESS CODE

The next essay on the topic of a school dress code is definitely above average. It would certainly receive a passing grade. It is also a good model for you to look at and think about in preparation for writing your own essay that examines advantages and disadvantages.

(1)   Our school is thinking about a dress code so that students would dress properly for school. For example, with a dress code you can't wear T-shirts that advertise beer or cigarettes. Also, you can't get your hair cut in certain ways or wear just any kind of shoes. Those are some of the things a dress code tells you about what you can wear to school.

(2)   Some of the good points about having a dress code are that people respect you when you dress properly. If you wear anything you want, people don't think you're serious about school. When you go to a party, you dress up for it. When you go to a job interview, you dress properly too. You look like you mean to be there. And everyone treats you that way.

(3)   Another good point is that you don't have fights with your mother about what to wear to school every day. Also, you can save money for your family by not wanting something different to wear all the time. When you're not dressing in the latest fad, you don't need as many clothes.

(4)   On the other hand, what if it's a very hot day and you want to wear something comfortable? If the dress code says you can't wear shorts, you'll be pretty uncomfortable all day. When you are uncomfortable, you can't concentrate, and your school work might suffer. Another bad point is that you will always have to think about the dress code before you buy a T-shirt or get a haircut. You'll have to think about what you are doing when you get dressed in the morning.

(5)   So these are some of the things I think are good and bad about a dress code. Other students might think of different things, but there will always be two sides to this question.

Analyzing a Successful Essay

Use this evaluation form to help you find out what strategies the writer used to make the essay successful.

▲ The Opening: Paragraph 1

Does the writer give you a clear idea of what this essay will be about? _____

Does the opening of the essay get your attention? _____

The writer begins this essay in an interesting way—by defining the term "dress code." The definition is followed by several examples that readers are sure to recognize. The examples also let the readers know what the essay will be about.

▲ The Body: Paragraphs 2, 3, and 4

Is there a clear organizational pattern? _____

Does the writer discuss both sides—the advantages and the disadvantages—of the topic? _____

Are there enough details so that the reader understands both the advantages and disadvantages? _____

Does the writer stick to the topic? _____

Does the writer use transitional words to indicate the contrast between the advantages and the disadvantages? _____

Does the writer use transitional words to connect ideas? _____

Do the word choice and sentence structure help make the composition interesting?

ELABORATION

Paragraphs 2, 3, and 4 are the body of the essay. They provide the specific details that explain what is good and what is bad about a dress code. For each general statement about something that is good or bad, the writer elaborates with a detail or an example.

In Paragraph 2, for instance, the writer gives one reason that having a dress code is a good thing: People respect you when you dress properly. This reason is supported with two examples—dressing up for a party and dressing up for a job interview.

Paragraph 3 provides additional good points supported by examples.

In Paragraph 4, the writer gives two reasons that having a dress code might be a bad thing and supports these reasons with examples.

ORGANIZATION

This kind of essay is easily organized by first discussing all the advantages (Paragraphs 2 and 3) then all the disadvantages (Paragraph 4).

Notice that Paragraph 4 begins with the phrase "on the other hand" to let the reader know that this paragraph is a contrast to what has gone before. The writer also uses transitional words and phrases like "another," "so," "also," and "but" to connect ideas.

Finally, there are no digressions. Every sentence is related to the writer's main idea.

LANGUAGE CONTROL

The structure of the sentences in this essay and the writer's choice of words is interesting and varied. The grammar, spelling, and punctuation are also correct.

AUDIENCE

The writer's language makes it clear that this essay has been written to inform an adult.

▲ The Closing

Does the essay have a strong closing? _____

The closing paragraph says clearly that the writer has come to the end of the essay and reminds the readers that there are two sides to the question of a dress code.

Notice that the writer does not take a position or give an opinion. The job of this kind of essay is to report, not to persuade.

16

Writing and Evaluating Your Own Essay

Topic: SUMMER SCHOOL

You are going to write an essay of your own, using the prompt below.

> Many schools have summer programs that include both academic courses like math and reading and special courses like band and computers. There are both good things and bad things about going to summer school.
>
> Write an essay for your teacher in which you explain both the advantages and the disadvantages of summer school. Be sure to explain each point fully.

Reading the Prompt

Follow the steps below to help you read this prompt. They will also give you a head start on planning and organizing your essay.

Step 1: READ THE PROMPT

What advantages and disadvantages come immediately to mind? _____

_____

_____

Step 2: IDENTIFY THE TASK

What am I supposed to do?

- What topic do I have to write about? _____

_____

Steps continue on the next page . . .

- What is the purpose of my essay? _____

  _____

- Who is my audience? _____

  _____

Step 3: READ BETWEEN THE LINES

What other facts might I need to answer this question? _____

_____

Step 4: USE PERSONAL EXPERIENCE

What do I know about this topic?

- Can I tell about an experience of my own? _____

- Can I tell about an experience someone else has had? _____

- Have I read about this topic or seen something about it on TV? _____

Step 5: REVIEW INITIAL THOUGHTS AND IDEAS

Do I want to make any new points? _____

_____

Do I want to take out any of the points I first thought of? _____

_____

Mapping the Essay

Complete the steps below to finish planning your essay.

1. Have you ever attended a summer school program? _____

   _____

   If so, what kind? _____

   _____

2. What did you like about it? _____

   _____

3. What did you not like about it? _____

_____

4. What are some of the reasons it might be a good idea to go to summer school? Whenever you can, use examples from your own experience or ones you have heard about.

_____

_____

5. What are some of the reasons it might not be a good idea to go to summer school? Whenever you can, use examples from your own experience or ones you have heard about.

_____

_____

6. Write some transitional words or phrases that you might use to show the contrast between the advantages and the disadvantages.

_____

_____

7. Jot down one or two ideas for your opening and one or two ideas for your closing. Try to think of something that would catch your readers' attention. Avoid using the same words and phrases in the opening and the closing.

Opening: _____

Closing: _____

Writing the First Draft

Use the mapping activities to write a first draft of your essay. Write your draft on a separate sheet of paper.

Evaluating and Improving Your Essay

When you have finished your draft, read what you have written. Ask yourself the following questions as you read. Check the appropriate boxes and write any comments on the lines provided. You can work on your own or with a partner.

1. Does the writer give you a clear idea of what this essay will be about?

    ☐ yes ☐ no   Comments: _____

2. Does the opening of the essay get your attention?

    ☐ yes ☐ no   Comments: _____

3. Is there a clear organizational pattern?

    ☐ yes ☐ no   Comments: _____

4. Does the writer discuss both sides of the topic—both the advantages and the disadvantages?

    ☐ yes ☐ no   Comments: _____

5. Are there enough details so that the reader understands both the advantages and the disadvantages?

    ☐ yes ☐ no   Comments: _____

6. Does the writer stick to the topic?

    ☐ yes ☐ no   Comments: _____

7. Does the writer use transitional words to indicate the contrast between the advantages and the disadvantages?

    ☐ yes ☐ no   Comments: _____

8. Do the word choice and sentence structure help make the essay interesting?

    ☐ yes ☐ no   Comments: _____

9. Is this essay appropriate for the stated audience?

    ☐ yes ☐ no   Comments: _____

10. Does the essay have a clear closing?

    ☐ yes ☐ no   Comments: _____

Decide what changes would improve your essay, and make these changes on your paper. Remember that these sorts of improvements can make a difference in your grade.

For extra practice, make a final copy of your revised essay. This time, make sure that the grammar, punctuation, and spelling are all correct.

17

Analyzing a Successful Essay

Topic: FAST FOOD

In this section, you will have another chance to analyze a successful essay that discusses advantages and disadvantages.

Here is the prompt you will be working with.

> Fast food restaurants have been gaining in popularity around the world. There are both good and bad things about fast food.
>
> Write a composition for your teacher in which you explain both what is good and what is bad about fast food. Be sure to explain each point fully.

Below is an essay written in response to this prompt. This is a successful essay—one that would receive an above-average grade. Read the essay; then answer the questions that follow to analyze what makes this essay successful.

(1)   What does your family do when they want a good, quick meal? They probably head for the nearest fast food restaurant—for hamburgers, fried chicken, or pizza. There are a lot of good things about fast food, most of all because it is fast. But there are also some disadvantages that you should think about before you order fries and a shake again.

(2)   Probably the best thing about fast food is that you get it quickly. You don't have to wait for a table or for someone to come to your table to take the order. Almost as soon as you order it, it's there, right in front of you. It also tastes pretty good. At least, it's the kind of food I like, and most places have enough things to choose from so that everybody can find something they like. For example, when we go out, my mom gets a grilled chicken sandwich, my dad gets fish, and my sister and I get burgers with everything on them. That brings me to another advantage of fast food. It doesn't cost too much. We can afford it one night a week when my mom and dad work late.

(3)   However, you might not want to eat it more than once a week. Although you can get salads in most places, the main part of the meal is usually greasy or fried. You can't get fresh vegetables like string beans or corn on the cob, and the only fruit is canned peaches in the salad bar. A lot of people on special diets for their health have a hard time finding anything that's all right for them to eat. My grandmother, for instance, can't eat fat or salt because of her heart. All she can eat usually is the grilled chicken sandwich without the sauce, which doesn't taste very good.

(4)   As you can see, fast food has both advantages and disadvantages. If you're thinking about saving time and not spending too much money, fast food will look good to you. But if you want something special, fast food isn't the answer.

Reader's Response

1. What do you think is good about this paper? Jot down one thing that you especially like. It could be a word, a phrase, or even a whole idea.

   _____

2. What would you like the writer of this paper to tell you more about?

   _____

Analyzing a Successful Essay

This essay can serve as a model for organizing your own essay. In addition, when you analyze it, you can find out what strategies the writer has used to make it essay successful.

▲ The Opening: Paragraph 1

Does the writer give you a clear idea of what this essay is about?

_____

Does the essay have a strong opening? For example, will it attract the reader's attention?

_____

The opening sentences get the reader's attention by asking and answering a question related to the topic. This is a good opening because it does not repeat the wording of the question. Following this question and answer, the writer states that there are both good and bad things to say about fast food and gives a specific example.

▲ *The Body: Paragraphs 2 and 3*

Is there a clear organizational pattern? _____

Does the writer discuss both sides of the topic—both the advantages and the disadvantages? _____

Are there enough details so that the reader understands both the advantages and disadvantages? _____

Does the writer stick to the topic? _____

Does the writer use transitional words to indicate the contrast between the advantages and the disadvantages? _____

Does the writer use transitional words to connect sentences with paragraphs?

_____

Do the word choice and sentence structure help make the essay interesting?

_____

Is this essay appropriate for the stated audience? _____

ELABORATION

Paragraphs 2 and 3 are the body of the essay. They provide the specific details that explain what is good and what is bad about fast food. For each general statement about something that is good or bad, the writer elaborates with a detail or an example.

In Paragraph 2, for instance, the writer tells exactly what each member of the family likes to eat. In Paragraph 3, the writer uses his/her grandmother as an example to explain why fast food can be a problem for some people.

ORGANIZATION

This kind of paper is easily organized by discussing all the advantages together in one paragraph and all the disadvantages in another. This writer only needed two paragraphs. If you have more details about either the advantages or the disadvantages, you can add a paragraph.

Notice that Paragraph 3 begins with the word "however" to let the reader know that what is coming up is a contrast to what has gone before. In addition, the writer uses transitional words and phrases like "for example," "although," "at least" and "for instance" to connect sentences within paragraphs.

Finally, there are no digressions; every sentence is related to the writer's main idea.

LANGUAGE CONTROL

The structure of the sentences in this essay and the writer's choice of words is interesting and varied. The grammar, spelling, and punctuation are also correct.

AUDIENCE

The writer's language makes it clear that this essay has been written to inform an adult.

▲ The Closing

Does the essay have a strong closing? For example, does it summarize the ideas already stated? _____

The closing paragraph uses a transitional phrase—"as you can see"—to introduce a summary of what is good and what is bad about fast food—This summary repeats the ideas stated in the body without repeating the exact words.

Notice that the writer does not take a position or give an opinion. The job of this kind of essay is to report, not to persuade.

18
Writing and Evaluating Your Own Essay

Topic: VOLUNTEER WORK

Here is a final chance to write an essay of your own that examines advantages and disadvantages. Your essay will be written in response to the prompt below.

> Many organizations in your community—hospitals, parks, schools, libraries—depend on volunteers. Your school is thinking of requiring all students to do some volunteer work in the community. There are advantages and disadvantages to requiring volunteer work.
>
> Write an essay for your principal in which you explain both what is good and what is bad about obligatory volunteer work. Be sure to explain each point fully.

Reading the Prompt

Follow the steps below to help you read the prompt and plan your essay.

Step 1: READ THE PROMPT

What are my first thoughts? _____

_____

What ideas come to mind? _____

_____

Use the list on the next page to organize your ideas.

VOLUNTEER WORK

GOOD POINTS	BAD POINTS
_____	_____
_____	_____
_____	_____
_____	_____

Step 2: IDENTIFY THE TASK

What am I supposed to do?

- What topic do I have to write about? _____

- What is the purpose of my essay? _____

- Who is my audience? _____

Step 3: READ BETWEEN THE LINES

What other facts might I need to answer this question? _____

Step 4: USE PERSONAL EXPERIENCE

What do I know about this topic?

- What are some of the good things I know about it? _____

- What are some of the bad things I know about it? _____

- Have I read about this topic or seen something about it on TV? _____

Step 5: REVIEW INITIAL THOUGHTS AND IDEAS

Do I want to add any new points? _____

_____

Do I want to take out any of the points I first thought of? _____

_____

_____

When you have finished this step, you will know what you think about the issue. You will also have begun to think about how you will elaborate your ideas.

Mapping the Essay

Complete the steps below to finish planning your essay.

1. What kinds of volunteer work have you done? _____

    _____

2. What other kinds of volunteer work do you know about in your community?

    _____

    _____

3. What are some of the reasons a school might require students to do volunteer

    work? _____

    _____

4. What are the advantages of required volunteer work? Whenever you can, use examples from your own experience or ones you have heard about.

    _____

    _____

5. What are some of the disadvantages of required volunteer work? Whenever you can, use examples from your own experience or ones you have heard about.

    _____

    _____

6. Write some transitional words or phrases that you might use to show the contrast between the advantages and the disadvantages.

   _____

   _____

7. Jot down one or two ideas for your opening and one or two ideas for your closing. Try to think of something that would catch your readers' attention. Avoid using the same words and phrases in the opening and the closing.

   Opening: _____

   _____

   _____

   Closing: _____

   _____

   _____

Writing the First Draft

Use what you have written in these mapping activities to write a first draft of your essay. Write your draft on a separate sheet of paper.

Evaluating and Improving Your Essay

When you have finished your draft, read what you have written. Then use the following form to analyze your essay. Check the appropriate boxes and write any comments on the lines. You can work on your own or with a partner.

1. Does the writer give you a clear idea of what this essay will be about?

   ❏ yes ❏ no   Comments: _____

2. Does the essay have a strong opening?

   ❏ yes ❏ no   Comments: _____

3. Is there a clear organizational pattern?

   ❏ yes ❏ no   Comments: _____

4. Does the writer discuss both sides of the topic—both the advantages and the disadvantages?

   ❏ yes ❏ no   Comments: _____

5. Are there enough details so that the reader understands both the advantages and disadvantages?

   ❏ yes ❏ no   Comments: _____

6. Does the writer stick to the topic?

   ❏ yes ❏ no   Comments: _____

7. Does the writer use transitional words to indicate the contrast between the advantages and disadvantages? Does the writer use transitional words to connect sentences within paragraphs?

   ❏ yes ❏ no   Comments: _____

8. Do the word choice and sentence structure help make the essay interesting?

   ❏ yes ❏ no   Comments: _____

9. Is this essay appropriate for the stated audience?

   ❏ yes ❏ no   Comments: _____

10. Does the essay have a strong closing?

   ❏ yes ❏ no   Comments: _____

Decide what changes would improve your essay, and make these changes on your paper. Remember that these sorts of improvements can make a difference in your grade.

For extra practice, make a final copy of your revised composition. This time, make sure that the grammar, puncutation, and spelling are all correct.

UNIT THREE

THE PROBLEM-SOLUTION ESSAY

In a problem-solution essay, you examine possible solutions to a problem, then decide which is the best solution and why.

This kind of essay is actually a combination of the two other essay types you have worked with in this book:

- a **persuasive** essay, and
- an essay that discusses **advantages and disadvantages.**

In the **problem-solution** essay, you take a look at a problem and weigh possible solutions to it (usually two), discussing what is good and what is bad about each solution. Or you consider a proposed course of action and consider what its advantages and disadvantages are. You consider what the effects of Decision A would be, what the effects of Decision B would be, and so on. When you have examined the solutions, you make a recommendation by stating which solution you would choose and giving reasons to support your choice.

19

Critical Thinking

WAYS OF BEING REASONABLE

In real life, there is more than one possible solution to a problem. And each solution has consequences—its good points and its bad points. When people are deciding which solution to choose, they want to know what these good points and bad points are, so that they can make reasonable decisions.

In a democratic form of government people follow certain rules of discussion so that everyone can be heard and all points of view can be expressed. The good points and bad points of each solution are weighed, as well as the consequences of each of the suggested actions. When everything has been presented, the group chooses the most workable solution.

How do you persuade an audience that your position is the most reasonable one? You'll need to rely on critical thinking skills like the following:

- Using **common sense** to draw reasonable conclusions about events.

- Thinking about the **consequences,** or results that your actions or decisions might have.

- Using **fair language** to describe both points of view.

Common Sense

Imagine this. You are working in an office. It is 4:30 in the afternoon, and a messenger arrives with wet hair and a soaking wet jacket. He wipes the moisture off his face, then takes out a tissue and dries off his glasses. When he leaves, you open your drawer and take out—

- a pair of sunglasses?

- an umbrella?

Common sense helps you come to the reasonable conclusion that it is raining outside. It also reminds you that it is close to quitting time and it might still be raining when you go outside. The reasonable thing to do is to take an umbrella.

EXERCISE 1: Using Common Sense

Try using your head—your common sense—on the following situations. Choose the sentence (a, b, or c) that makes the most sense in the blank line. Write the letter of the sentence on the line.

1. Angela had missed a lot of school and was nervous about taking a test in her poorest subject. _____ . She did a lot better on this test than she had ever done before.

   a. She listened to soothing music when she studied the night before the exam.

   b. She asked to take the test as a makeup and got extra help.

   c. She stayed up all night studying.

2. _____ . The workers refused. A strike began.

   a. The factory wanted to save money by cutting worker's salaries.

   b. The factory tried to save money by retraining its workers.

   c. The company tried to save money by buying new machines.

3. Because of the threat of terrorism, many people did not want to fly. _____ _____ . Air travel went back to normal.

   a. Airlines cut their prices in half.

   b. The government said that there was nothing to worry about.

   c. Car rental companies lowered their prices in Europe and South America.

4. If the hole in the ozone layer gets larger, more humans will develop skin cancer. Recently, there has been an increase in the kind of pollution that destroys the ozone layer. _____ .

   a. Skin cancer can be expected to increase.

   b. The amount of skin cancer will remain the same.

   c. Skin cancer can be expected to decrease.

5. Anyone who fights on school property gets an automatic suspension. Chuck sees his friend Clifford fighting someone in the hallway. _____ .

   a. Chuck pretends that he doesn't see anything.

   b. Chuck goes to the office to report the incident.

   c. Chuck gets suspended.

Consequences

Finding a good solution to a problem involves thinking about the consequences of each action you might take.

Your friend Lara has a problem. When she was in a music store with her cousin last week, she saw her put a tape in her pocket without paying for it. What should Lara do about this situation?

Your conversation goes something like this:

You: Tell her you don't want to go to the mall.

Lara: She'll want to know why.

You: Tell her you saw what she did.

Lara: She'll get mad.

You: Tell her you'll go, but that you'll report her to the store manager if you see her take anything.

Lara: Maybe the manager will think I've been stealing too.

Every time you suggest something, Lara worries about the effects of the action. This kind of reaction is normal. It is also a good way to anticipate further problems. You and Lara decide to make a chart showing what you have talked about and what is most likely to happen as the result of each action.

EXERCISE 2: Determining Consequences

Complete the chart below, using the conversation between you and Lara as your source of information. Then add two new possible actions and their consequences.

PROBLEM: What to Do About Shoplifting Cousin

ACTION: *Tell her you don't want to go to the mall.*

CONSEQUENCES: *She'll want to know why.*

ACTION: _____

CONSEQUENCES: _____

ACTION: _____

CONSEQUENCES: _____

ACTION: _____

CONSEQUENCES: _____

ACTION: _____

CONSEQUENCES: _____

ACTION: _____

CONSEQUENCES: _____

EXERCISE 3: Solving Problems

Read the situations below. Imagine that you are the one who has to make the decision. As you think about what you might do, make a chart on a separate piece of paper to show the possible consequences of each step you consider taking. Each situation will give you hints, but you may want to think of other consequences as well.

1. You need to save money for college and have been offered two after-school jobs. One pays almost twice as much money as the other, but you must work 25 hours a week in order to keep the job. You also need to take another math course to be better prepared for college. However, math isn't your best subject, and you will need tutoring.

2. Your mother and father are getting a divorce and you have to decide which parent you want to live with. Your mother will be staying in the town you now live in. You have friends and the school isn't too bad. But you will be moving to a much smaller place, and you will have no room of your own. You will also have to take an after-school job to help with expenses. Your father has just rented a large house in another town. You will have a room of your own, and you won't have to work. However, you don't think the school in that town is very good.

3. Your new boyfriend/girlfriend wants to go steady. The parent you live with thinks that at your age going with one person is not a good idea. Your best friend says that going steady is great because you always have a date. One more thing: You are pretty sure that the boy/girl who sits next to you in history class is interested in you.

Fair Language

To help you and your audience make a decision based on reason, it is important to use fair, neutral language when you present each side. Using emotionally charged language for one side and not the other tells your reader which side you are on. It also says that you have already made up your mind and are not giving unbiased information.

EXERCISE 4: Using Neutral Language

A. Read each statement and identify the issue. Ask yourself:

- What is the real subject of the discussion?

- Can you tell which position the writer favors? Which words or phrases tell you this?

- Which statements are written in neutral language?

1. Any school which puts in a dress code for students is depriving them of their constitutional rights.

2. Some educators have reported that students who wear uniforms to school perform better on statewide tests and miss fewer days of school.

3. There is no question that the junk food consumed in fast-food restaurants by many people every day can lead to serious health problems.

4. A student who feels uncomfortable in school may find it hard to concentrate on learning.

5. Shorts and sandals belong on the beach, not in school.

6. Students have no right to demand that schools cater to every food whim.

7. As anyone who ever ate one knows, there is no such thing as a good school lunch.

8. Students have enough trouble passing courses they take for credit without having to worry about finding the time to do community service work for no pay and no grades.

9. Community services like the library, hospitals, playgrounds, and daycare centers couldn't do as much as they do without volunteer help.

10. Good nutrition, good value, and little waste is the goal of every school lunch program.

B. Rewrite five of the statements that are <u>not</u> in neutral language. Rewrite them so that you cannot tell what the writer's position on the issue is.

1. _____

_____

2. _____

_____

3. _____

_____

4. _____

_____

5. _____

_____

20
Analyzing a Successful Essay

Topic: FOOD SERVICE OPTIONS AT SCHOOL

Here is an example of a problem-solution prompt. Notice that it asks you to discuss two possibilities and to state which one you prefer.

> A new high school is being built for your district. The school board is considering two options for the food service at this school—using a traditional cafeteria-style service, or bringing in a fast-food restaurant to run the service.
>
> In a letter to the school board, discuss both possibilities, state which you prefer, and provide convincing reasons for your choice.

Below is an essay written in response to this prompt. This is a successful essay—one that would receive an above-average grade. Read the essay; then answer the questions that follow to analyze what makes this essay successful.

Dear Members of the School Board:

(1)   High school students have always complained about the food in the cafeteria. As one of those high school students, I am glad that the Board is considering two different possibilities for the new high school cafeteria. One is to have a traditional cafeteria-style service. The other is to bring in a fast-food restaurant to run the cafeteria. Here is what I think about this question.

(2)   It's true that there have been lots of complaints about the cafeteria in the past, but that doesn't mean that a cafeteria service couldn't be good. Cafeteria style offers lots of choices, including many fresh foods. You can get soups, salads of all kinds, different kinds of sandwiches, and daily hot specials. Cafeterias like Luby's or Shoney's always have many kinds of fresh vegetables and fruits. And if you like sweet things, there are great desserts. There is no reason that a good school cafeteria can't do the same thing. A menu like this would appeal to more students and it would be better for them. And it is well known that healthier students are better students. They have more energy and can concentrate better on their work.

(3)   Fast food, on the other hand, is very convenient. There aren't too many choices and everything is all prepared ahead of time, so you can get served quickly. Also, it tastes pretty good. It's the kind of food that most students like, and fast food places usually have enough things to choose from so that everybody can find something they like. One popular restaurant has grilled chicken sandwiches, fried fish, and salads, as well as burgers. Finally, it is probably cheaper for the school to run a fast-food service because the menu never changes and there isn't a big choice of foods.

(4)   Although there are some good things about fast foods, I don't think this kind of food service belongs in the high school. It would be better to have a well-run cafeteria that offers a variety of fresh foods. For one thing, you might not want to eat fast food every day of the week. Although you can get salads in most fast-food places, the main part of the meal is usually greasy or fried. You can't get fresh vegetables like string beans or corn on the cob, and the only fruit is canned peaches in the salad bar. In addition, if you're on a special diet, you have a hard time finding anything that's all right to eat.

(5)   With a good cafeteria-style service, you could provide not only food that students want to eat but food that is good for them. A healthier, happier student body would improve the athletic and academic standing of this school. I hope you will consider my recommendation. I would also like to suggest that you ask every student who will be going to the new high school to send in recommendations as well.

Sincerely,

▲ *Reader's Response*

1. What do you think is good about this paper? Write one thing that you especially like. It could be a word, a phrase, or even a whole idea.

_____

_____

2. What would you like the writer of this paper to tell you more about?

_____

_____

Analyzing a Successful Essay

This essay can serve as a model for organizing your own paper. When you analyze it, you will discover what strategies the writer has used to make the essay successful.

Remember: a Problem-Solution Essay uses parts of the two essays that you have already practiced writing. It discusses both the advantages and the disadvantages of something. It also takes a position and presents convincing reasons to support that position.

Notice how the essay is organized.

▲ *The Opening: Paragraph 1*

In the first two sentences, the writer establishes his/her involvement in the issue, then goes on to state what the issue is and what two courses of action have been recommended. Notice that the writer's position is not given in the first paragraph.

▲ *The Body: Paragraphs 2-4*

PARAGRAPH 2

Here the writer discusses the first option—cafeteria-style service. The paragraph begins by answering an objection to this option that would probably be in the minds of many readers. He/she continues by discussing what is good about cafeteria-style service. The three reasons given—choice, freshness, and health—are supported by many details and personal examples. The paragraph closes with a benefit statement that will appeal to the intended audience.

PARAGRAPH 3

This paragraph is similar in construction to Paragraph 2. The second option is introduced, with a transitional phrase that indicates the contrast between the two choices. The writer then continues by discussing what is good about fast-food style service. The reasons given—convenience, popularity, and lower costs—are, like the reasons in Paragraph 2, supported by many details. This paragraph also closes with a benefit statement intended to appeal to members of the school board.

Notice that many of the details in this paragraph are the same as those used in the successful essay that discussed the advantages and disadvantages of fast food.

PARAGRAPH 4

The final paragraph of the body of the essay gives the writer's position—that cafeteria-style service is preferable to fast-food service. The writer supports this position by explaining what is bad about fast food.

Notice again that many of the details in this paragraph are the same as those used in the successful essay that discussed the advantages and disadvantages of fast food.

▲ *The Closing*

The closing begins by restating the writer's main point in an interesting way. The writer than adds a new reason that has special appeal for the audience and finishes by making a reasonable and useful suggestion.

21
Writing and Evaluating Your Own Essay

Topic: COMMUNITY VOLUNTEER WORK OPTIONS

Now you are going to write an essay of your own that discusses solutions to a problem. Your essay will be written in response to the prompt below.

> Your school has decided that a semester of volunteer work would benefit both the students and the community. The principal is considering two ways of implementing a program of required volunteer work. One way is for the school to assign students to a volunteer job during an extra period at the end of the school day. The other is to let students make a commitment of five hours a week to a volunteer job of their choice.
>
> In a letter to your principal, discuss both options, state your position, and provide convincing reasons for your position.

Reading the Prompt

Follow the steps below to help you read the prompt and plan your essay.

Step 1: READ THE PROMPT

How do I feel about this question/situation? What is my position? _____

_____

_____

Step 2: IDENTIFY THE TASK

What am I supposed to do?

• What question/issue am I supposed to address? _____

_____

- What are the two courses of action? _____

_____

- What is the purpose of my essay? _____

_____

- Who is my audience? _____

_____

Step 3: READ BETWEEN THE LINES

What other facts might I need to answer this question? _____

_____

Step 4: USE PERSONAL EXPERIENCE

What do I know about this topic?

- Can I tell about an experience of my own? _____

- Can I tell about an experience someone else has had? _____

- Have I heard or read about this issue or situation or seen something about it on TV? _____

Step 5: FORM A FINAL OPINION

How do I feel about this question/issue now? _____

_____

_____

Mapping the Essay

Now take out the essay you wrote in which you discussed the advantages and disadvantages of required volunteer work. In the following activities and in your new essay, re-use whatever you can.

1. List everything that is good about school-assigned volunteer work.

_____

_____

Use these details to write either Paragraph 2 or Paragraph 3 of your essay.

2. List everything that is good about student-selected volunteer work.

   _____

   _____

   Use these details to write either Paragraph 2 or Paragraph 3 of your essay.

3. List as many reasons as you can think of for supporting the position you have taken.

   _____

   _____

   Use these reasons to write Paragraph 4 of your essay.

4. Make some notes for ideas you can use in your opening paragraph and your closing paragraph. It's always a good idea to include reasons and suggestions that your audience will think of as benefits.

   Opening _____

   _____

   Closing _____

   _____

Writing the First Draft

Use what you have written in these mapping activities to write a first draft of your essay. Write your draft on a separate sheet of paper.

Evaluating and Improving the Essay

When you have finished your draft, read what you have written. Then use the following form to analyze your essay. Check the appropriate boxes and write any comments on the lines. You can work on your own or with a partner.

1. Does the writer give you a clear idea of what the two courses of action are?

   ❏ yes ❏ no Comments: _____

2. Does the writer explain each of the possible courses of action, backing them up with details and examples?

   ❏ yes ❏ no Comments: _____

3. Does the writer state his or her position clearly and support it with examples?

   ❏ yes ❏ no Comments: _____

4. Does the writer choose reasons that are sound?

   ❏ yes ❏ no Comments: _____

5. Do the opening and closing introduce and summarize the ideas clearly?

   ❏ yes ❏ no Comments: _____

Decide what changes would improve your essay, and make these changes on your paper. Remember that these sorts of improvements can make a difference in your grade.

For extra practice, make a final copy of your revised essay. This time, make sure that the grammar, punctuation, and spelling are all correct.

UNIT FOUR

THE HOW-TO ESSAY

In school or on a test, you may be asked to write an essay in which you tell somebody how to do something. It is usually something you already know how to do, so it is easy to use your own experience to write this kind of essay. What matters is how well you can write instructions.

22

Analyzing a Successful Essay

Topic: YOUR PET "TRADE SECRET"

Here is the first prompt you will be working with.

> After a few years on the job, everyone acquires some trade secrets—techniques that make the job easier to do. Your job for the last few years has been to be a student.
>
> Write a composition in which you tell another student about a technique you have learned that helps you succeed either in a specific course or in a specific school activity.

Below is an example of a successful model composition written in response to this prompt. After reading it, you will analyze what makes it successful. Then you will learn strategies for planning, writing, evaluating, and improving your own composition.

(1)   What's the hardest thing a student has to do in high school? Most people would say it's writing a paper. Since there's no way to get out of this job, it makes sense to learn an efficient way of getting your thoughts down on paper. I use a series of steps called the writing process. This is a method I learned in seventh grade. It helps me figure out what I want to say and how I want to say it.

(2)   First make sure you know what the assignment is. Then write down everything you know about the topic. You don't have to worry about your spelling or about writing complete sentences. Then look at what you've written. Can you put your ideas into groups? Draw lines to connect ideas or circle or number your ideas to show which ones go together. This part of the process is called prewriting.

(3)   The next step is writing. Figuring out a good opening is worth spending time on. I try to tell about something that happened to me or to a friend that I can connect with the topic. For example, once when I had to write about what the legal driving age should be, I began with a story about my cousin, who was a good driver when

he was only twelve years old. Then I try to say in general what my essay is going to be about. After that, I write a paragraph about each group of ideas.

(4)   After writing comes revising. This is when you re-read what you have written and decide what to change. Sometimes you need to add things. Sometimes you need to take things out. Sometimes something doesn't make sense, and you have to figure out a different way of saying it. It's pretty hard to know what to change, so I like to ask someone else to read what I've written.

(5)   The last step doesn't seem so big, but it can make a big difference in your grade. This is editing. Go over your paper very carefully and correct every mistake you find. Get everything right before you copy it over in your best handwriting. If your handwriting is so bad that no one can read it, maybe it's time to learn to type.

(6)   I can't guarantee that your next essay will get an A, but these ideas should make the job of writing it much easier.

▲ Reader's Response

1. What do you think is good about this paper? Write one thing that you especially like. It could be a word, a phrase, or even a whole idea.

    _____

    _____

2. What would you like the writer of this paper to tell you more about?

    _____

    _____

Analyzing a Successful Essay

The sample essay can serve as a model for organizing your own essay. In addition, when you analyze the model, you can find out what strategies the writer used to make it successful.

▲ The Opening: Paragraph 1

Does the writer give you a clear idea of what this essay will be about?

_____

Does the opening attract the reader's attention? _____

The opening sentence gets the readers' attention by asking a question. In the next few sentences, the writer names a task that is difficult for high school students—writing a paper—and says that he/she has a method for coping with this task. Finally, the writer identifies the method and explains briefly why it works.

▲ The Body: Paragraphs 2-5

Are there enough details so that the reader understands each step? _____

Are the steps described in the order in which the writer does them? _____

Does each paragraph describe a different step? _____

Are transitional words used to indicate when each step is done? _____

Does the writer stick to the topic? _____

Do the word choice and sentence structure help make the essay interesting? _____

Is the essay appropriately worded for the audience? _____

ELABORATION

Paragraphs 2-5 are the body of the essay. The steps for writing a paper are described in this part of the essay. Notice that the writer covers all the steps and includes enough details so that someone else could follow the same method. For example, in Paragraph 2, the writer describes several ways to group ideas. In Paragraph 3, the writer gives an example of an interesting opening.

Whenever possible, the writer also explains why he/she does certain things. For example, in Paragraph 5, the writer states that editing is important because it can make a big difference in your grade.

ORGANIZATION

Paragraphs 2-5 describe the writing process in an order that makes sense. In this case, it means giving the steps in the order in which you do them. Each paragraph describes a separate step or group of steps to make the process easier to follow. The steps are connected by transitional words or phrases that also help make the order clear—for example, *first, then, the next step, after, the last step.*

Finally, the writer sticks to the topic. There are no digressions—sentences that bring up new, unrelated ideas.

LANGUAGE CONTROL

The structure of the sentences in this essay and the writer's choice of words is interesting and varied. The grammar, spelling, and punctuation are also correct.

AUDIENCE

The writer's informal language makes it clear that this essay has been written to help another student.

▲ The Closing

Does the essay have a strong closing? For example, does the reader have a sense

that the writer is finished? _____

The closing does not have to be long. This writer has written only one sentence, but it is humorous, addresses the audience, and leaves the reader with the sense that the essay is complete.

23
Writing and Evaluating Your Own Essay

Topic: YOUR PET "TRADE SECRET"

You are going to write an essay of your own, using the same prompt.

> After a few years on the job, everyone acquires some trade secrets—techniques that make the job easier to do. Your job for the last few years has been to be a student.
>
> Write an essay in which you tell another student about a technique you have learned that helps you succeed either in a specific course or in a specific school activity.

Reading the Prompt

Follow the steps below to help you read the prompt and plan your essay.

Step 1: READ THE PROMPT

What do I think I want to write about? _____

_____

_____

Step 2: IDENTIFY THE TASK

What am I supposed to do?

• What kind of activity am I supposed to be telling about? _____

_____

• What is the purpose of my essay? _____

_____

• Who is my audience? _____

_____

Step 3: USE PERSONAL EXPERIENCE

Which activity do I know the most about?

• Can I visualize myself doing this activity? _____

• Is it possible to describe this activity clearly on paper? _____

Step 4: REVIEW INITIAL THOUGHTS AND IDEAS

Have I changed my mind about which activity to write about? _____

_____

_____

Mapping the Essay

Complete the steps below to finish planning your composition.

1. List all the steps someone must follow in order to use the technique you are describing.

   _____

   _____

2. Look at your list. See if you can group the steps into paragraphs for the body of the composition. Put an **A** next to all the steps that belong in the first paragraph of the body, a **B** next to all the steps that belong in the next paragraph, and so on. You will probably have three or four paragraphs.

3. Look at the paragraph groups and decide what the main idea of each group is. For example, in the model composition, the main idea of Paragraph 2 is prewriting. Write the main idea of each of your paragraph groups below.

   Paragraph A _____

   Paragraph B _____

   Paragraph C _____

   Other (if you have more than three paragraphs in the body) _____

   _____

4. Decide what order you want to put the paragraphs in, and number each main idea to show the order.

5. Write some transitional words or phrases that you might use to show the connections between paragraphs or to introduce paragraphs.

   Paragraph 1 _____

   Paragraph 2 _____

   Paragraph 3 _____

   Other _____

   _____

6. Jot down one or two ideas for your opening and one or two ideas for your closing.

   Opening: _____

   _____

   _____

   Closing: _____

   _____

   _____

Writing the First Draft

Use what you have written in these mapping activities to write a first draft of your essay. Write your draft on a separate sheet of paper.

Evaluating and Improving the Essay

When you have finished your draft, read what you have written. Then use the following form to analyze your essay. Check the appropriate boxes and write any comments on the lines. You can work on your own or with a partner.

1. Does the writer give you a clear idea of what this essay will be about?
   ❑ yes ❑ no Comments: _____

2. Does the essay have a strong opening? Why or why not?
   ❑ yes ❑ no Comments: _____

3. Are there enough details so that the reader understands each step?
   ❑ yes ❑ no Comments: _____

4. Are the steps described in the order in which a person does them?
   ❑ yes ❑ no Comments: _____

5. Does each paragraph describe a different step?
   ❑ yes ❑ no Comments: _____

6. Are transitional words used to indicate when each step is done?
   ❑ yes ❑ no Comments: _____

7. Does the writer stick to the topic?
   ❑ yes ❑ no Comments: _____

8. Do the word choice and sentence structure help make the essay interesting?
   ❑ yes ❑ no Comments: _____

9. Is this essay appropriate for the stated audience?
   ❑ yes ❑ no Comments: _____

10. Does the essay have a strong closing? Why or why not?
   ❑ yes ❑ no Comments: _____

Decide what changes would improve your essay, and make these changes on your paper. Remember that on the test, these sorts of improvements can raise your score.

For extra practice, make a final copy of your revised essay. This time, make sure that the grammar, punctuation, and spelling are all correct.

UNIT FIVE

THE DESCRIPTIVE ESSAY

In school or on a test, you may be asked to write a descriptive essay. This means that you will be asked to describe something that you have seen or done. Whatever you choose, you will be expected to describe it so clearly and fully that your readers will feel as though they were there.

24

Analyzing a Successful Essay

Topic: AN EXTRACURRICULAR ACTIVITY

Here is the prompt you will be working with.

> Your school is producing a handbook that describes all the extracurricular activities, teams, and clubs that students can join.

> Select an activity, team, or club with which you are familiar and describe it in detail.

Below is an example of a model essay written in response to this prompt. After reading it, you will analyze what makes it successful. Then you will learn strategies for planning, writing, evaluating, and improving your own essay.

(1)   The drama club at our school is open to every student who wants to be involved in putting on plays. We have actors, singers, and dancers, of course. But they make up only half the club. The rest of the club is made up of students who design and build sets, set up and run the lights, and design and make the costumes. For plays, there is also a makeup crew, a stage crew, and sometimes an orchestra.

(2)   Mr. Zaleski and Mrs. Wade are the faculty advisors. They help us choose the plays, and they take turns directing them. Mr. Martinez, the shop teacher, is in charge of all the technical crews and supervises the building of the sets. The faculty also helps us with fund-raising, and so do many of the parents. We use the money we raise this way and the money we get from selling tickets to the shows to buy scripts and materials for sets and costumes.

(3)   We put on two plays every year—one musical and one non-musical. You have to audition to be in them. Actors think they have the toughest auditions because they have to read from the play without seeing it ahead of time. But singers and dancers say their job is tougher. They have to prepare something to perform for the audition. Either way, everyone is always so nervous that they look like they're going to be sick.

(4)   Finally, the results of the auditions are posted on the bulletin board. Some people are too scared to look and ask other people to look for them. You know who who has got the parts they wanted by the shouts of excitement and congratulations. Then the hard work begins—rehearsals, production meetings, sewing costumes, finding props, choreographing the dance routines. All this time, you still have to go to classes, do your homework, and keep your grades up.

(5)   The last two nights before the play opens are the tech rehearsal and the dress rehearsal. At the tech rehearsal, the actors don't say any lines. They just practice entrances and exits to get the curtains and the lights and the set changes coordinated. The dress rehearsal is like the real thing, complete with costumes and make-up. It's usually a disaster, but theater people always say that a bad dress rehearsal means a great opening night. In any case, our opening nights always are great. When the curtain comes down and the audience starts to applaud, all of a sudden we know we did everything just right.

▲ *Reader's Response*

1. What do you think is good about this paper? Write one thing that you especially like. It could be a word, a phrase, or even a whole idea.

   _____

   _____

2. What would you like the writer of this paper to tell you more about?

   _____

   _____

Analyzing a Successful Essay

This essay can help you organize your own essay. When you analyze it, you can find out what strategies the writer has used to make this essay successful.

▲ *The Opening: Paragraph*

The writer begins by naming the club he/she is going to describe. The rest of the paragraph tells something about the purpose of the club and who belongs to it.

▲ *The Body: Paragraphs 2-4*

PARAGRAPH 2

This paragraph names the faculty members involved in the club and tells what they do. As part of this description, the writer explains how the club raises money to support its activities.

PARAGRAPH 3

Specific details about the club's major activities are given in this paragraph. Here the writer begins to use more vivid language to communicate the tension and excitement surrounding auditions.

PARAGRAPH 4

The writer begins this paragraph by making a transition from auditions to production. Again, vivid language and specific details are used to make the events and feelings described more immediate to the reader.

▲ *The Closing*

Continuing to follow the chronological sequence established in paragraphs 3 and 4, the writer describes the activities that lead up to opening night. Here the writer details some of the behind-the-scenes activities of the tech rehearsal and dress rehearsal. The last two sentences conclude the essay by describing some of the feelings that motivate students to join the drama club.

25
Writing and Evaluating Your Own Essay

Topic: AN EXTRACURRICULAR ACTIVITY

You are going to write an essay of your own, using the same prompt.

> Your school is producing a handbook that describes all the extra-curricular activities, teams, and clubs that students can join.

> Select an activity, team, or club with which you are familiar and describe it in detail.

Reading the Prompt

Follow the steps below to help you read the prompt and plan your essay.

Step 1: READ THE PROMPT

What ideas come to mind? What do I think I want to write about? _____

_____

_____

Step 2: IDENTIFY THE TASK

What am I supposed to do?

- What kind of activity am I supposed to be telling about? _____

  _____

- What is the purpose of my essay? _____

  _____

- Who is my audience? _____

_____

Step 3: USE PERSONAL EXPERIENCE

Which activity do I know the most about?

- What do I think is most interesting about this activity? _____

_____

- Is it possible to describe this activity clearly on paper? _____

Step 4: REVIEW INITIAL THOUGHTS AND IDEAS

Have I changed my mind about which activity to write about? _____

_____

_____

Mapping the Essay

Complete the steps below to finish planning your essay.

1. Answer the following questions. Use the answers to write Paragraphs 1 and 2 of your essay.

   What is the name of the club/activity/team? _____

   Who are the members? How do they join? _____

   _____

   Who are the faculty advisors? What do they do? _____

   _____

   How do you raise money for the club/activity/team? _____

   _____

2. What is the major activity of this group? Visualize this activity and some of the preparation that goes into it. (It might help to close your eyes while you do this.) Then make some notes based on what you have visualized. Here are some things you might want to include:

        specific actions   facial expressions   tone of voice

        background sounds   special clothing

Use these notes to write the rest of the body of your essay.

3. Make some notes for ideas you can use in your opening and closing. Remember that you can get the reader's attention with a question, a dramatic situation, or a piece of interesting information.

Opening: _____

_____

_____

Closing: _____

_____

_____

Writing the First Draft

Use what you have written in these mapping activities to write a first draft of your essay. Write your draft on a separate sheet of paper.

Evaluating and Improving the Essay

When you have finished your draft, read what you have written. Then use the following form to analyze your essay. Check the appropriate boxes and write any comments on the lines. You can work on your own or with a partner.

1. Does the writer begin with a clear statement of what the activity/club/team is and who can join it?

   ❏ yes ❏ no Comments: _____

2. Does the writer describe this group's major activity with enough detail to give the reader a clear picture?

   ❏ yes ❏ no Comments: _____

3. Are the details of the description grouped in a way that makes sense?

   ❏ yes ❏ no Comments: _____

4. Does the writer use interesting language that makes the description come alive for the reader?

   ❏ yes ❏ no Comments: _____

5. Does the opening attract the reader's attention? Does the closing let the reader know that the essay is finished?

   ❏ yes ❏ no Comments: _____

Decide what changes would improve your essay, and make these changes on your paper. Remember that on the test, these sorts of improvements can often raise your score.

For extra practice, make a final copy of your revised essay. This time, make sure that the grammar, punctuation, and spelling are all correct.

PART TWO

SENTENCE CONSTRUCTION, USAGE, AND MECHANICS

PART TWO

INTRODUCTION

Most writing tests are in two parts. One part consists of short passages followed by multiple-choice questions on correct sentence formation, usage, spelling, capitalization, and punctuation. It is discussed in this section of *The Writing Test.*

Multiple-choice writing test questions test your knowledge. You must know how to form sentences correctly. You must be familiar with the rules of correct English usage. You must know how to spell correctly, and how to capitalize and punctuate a written passage. You are being tested on your knowledge of these rules and your ability to spot errors in all these areas.

26

Sentence Construction

Here are some basic things you should know about sentence construction:

- A *sentence* is a group of words that expresses a complete thought and that contains a subject and a predicate.

- The *subject* of a sentence is the word or group of words that tells who or what is doing the action of the sentence, or who or what the sentence is about.

- The *predicate* is the part of the sentence that tells what the subject is <u>doing</u> or what the subject <u>is.</u> It contains the verb of the sentence.

Here are some examples of simple sentences:

SUBJECT	PREDICATE
Maria . . .	. . . won the election easily.

SUBJECT	PREDICATE
A twister . . .	. . . is a highly destructive storm.

You can form more complicated sentences by combining two or more simple sentences, or by adding on phrases, dependent (subordinate) clauses, etc. But sometimes sentences are combined wrongly, or an add-on phrase or clause is punctuated as if it were a sentence. These are the kinds of mistakes you are often tested on. Be especially careful of *sentence fragments* and *run-on sentences.*

Sentence Fragments (Incomplete Sentences)

A *sentence fragment* is a group of words that is actually only part of a sentence, but that is punctuated like a true sentence, with a capital at the beginning and a period at the end. Another name for a fragment is *incomplete sentence.*

There are many kinds of sentence fragments. Two of the most common are *phrases* and *dependent clauses.*

PHRASES. One kind of sentence fragment consists of prepositional phrases, verbal phrases, subjects without verbs, and even predicates alone, punctuated like sentences. For example:

Without a glance in my direction.	*(prepositional phrases)*
Having waited for over an hour.	*(verbal phrase plus prepositional phrase)*
A dusty red car with one headlight.	*(subject alone, without a predicate)*
Gave it his best effort.	*(predicate, but no subject)*

▲ *Practice*

Pick out the sentence fragments.

   a. In the silence after the storm.

   b. A star was glowing in the evening sky just above the horizon.

   c. Picking his way carefully down the mountain.

   d. Edward left.

   e. Before long, a sound in the distance.

   f. A field of bluebonnets rippling in a gentle breeze.

DEPENDENT OR SUBORDINATE CLAUSES. Another kind of fragment consists of a group of words with a subject and a predicate (like a sentence), but introduced by words like **when, if, because, although, after, before, who, which,** etc. A dependent clause must always be attached to another sentence. It should never be punctuated like a sentence itself. So all of the following are sentence fragments:

Because of the unusual weather conditions.

After we finished raking the yard.

As if he didn't know better.

Although she could have afforded it.

Which has stood in this spot for a century.

▲ *Practice*

Pick out the sentence fragments.

   g. When night falls, bats swoop through the darkening sky.

   h. When night falls.

   i. As the ball sailed overhead, Ray made a flying leap.

   j. Ray made a flying leap.

   k. Which came roaring down the tracks toward us.

Run-On Sentences

A *run-on sentence* consists of two or more sentences that are joined together without the proper punctuation or without a conjunction (a joining word like **and, or, but, nor, for, yet**).

NO PUNCTUATION. One kind of run-on sentence consists of sentences that are run together without any punctuation at all:

> I threw James the ball he dropped it.
> (*Correct*: I threw James the ball. He dropped it.)

> The traffic sped past there was no place to cross.
> (*Correct:* The traffic sped past. There was no place to cross.)

COMMA SPLICE. A second kind of run-on sentence consists of two sentences joined only by a comma (without a conjunction). Here are the example sentences above, written with comma splices:

> I threw James the ball, he dropped it.

> The traffic sped past, there was no place to cross.

You can correct a run-on sentence with a semicolon, but not with a comma. (Both the part before the semicolon and the part after it have to be good sentences, however.)

▲ Practice

Pick out the run-on sentences.

   l. The Owls won the game, they outscored the Panthers by ten points.

   m. The doorbell rang suddenly Marla jumped.

   n. I read that book, you'll like it.

   o. We waited for an hour; Marvin never arrived.

   p. In the 1930's, rain stopped falling in the western plains, and rich wheat farms became empty stretches of dust.

Strategies and Tips

1. Remember the basic definition of a sentence:

> *A sentence is a group of words—*
>
> > *—that expresses a complete thought, and*
> >
> > *—that contains a subject and a predicate.*

2. You must be able to recognize the two kinds of badly constructed sentences that you may be tested on:

A. *A sentence fragment* is an incomplete sentence. It lacks a subject or a predicate. Common kinds of fragments are *phrases* and *dependent* (or *subordinate*) *clauses.* (If you forget what these are, go to the second page of this chapter and read about them.)

B. *A run-on sentence* consists of two sentences that are joined together without the proper punctuation or without a conjunction. A run-on sentence may have no punctuation at all between the two sentence parts. Or the sentence parts may be joined by a comma alone, in which case the sentence error is called a *comma splice*.

27

Sentence Combining

Here are some basic things you should be able to do when you combine sentences:

A. Fix fragments and run-on sentences.

B. Combine sentences or sentence parts in different ways.

This section will show you how to do each of these.

Fixing Fragments and Run-on Sentences

FIXING SENTENCE FRAGMENTS. A sentence fragment, or incomplete sentence, usually belongs with the sentence before it or after it. So to cure a fragment problem, combine the fragment with the sentence it belongs to:

Sentence plus fragment: Janet watched the waves. Beating against the shore.

Correct: Janet watched the waves beating against the shore.

▲ *Practice*

Rewrite each of the following to remove the fragments.

a. I'd like a hamburger. With onions and pickles. _____

_____

b. Sam did not come to town with us. Because he missed the bus. _____

_____

c. One of the earliest television stars was J. Fredd Muggs. Who was a chimpanzee.

_____

_____

FIXING RUN-ON SENTENCES. There are several ways to fix a run-on sentence. Here are some of the most common ones:

1. Separate the sentence parts into two sentences:

    Run-on: Nancy pressed the switch all the lights went out.

    Correct: Nancy pressed the switch. All the lights went out.

2. Join the sentence parts with a comma plus a conjunction like *and, or, but, yet,* etc. This kind of sentence is a **compound sentence.**

    Run-on: Hank cooked the chili, he did not make dessert.

    Correct: Hank cooked the chili, **but** he did not make dessert.

3. Join the sentence parts with a semicolon:

    Run-on: Suzanna volunteered to take tickets tonight last night she sold programs.

    Correct: Suzanna volunteered to take tickets tonight; last night she sold programs.

4. Combine the sentence parts by using a relative pronoun (*which, who, whom,* or *that*) or a subordinating conjunction (*although, because, when, if, after, before,* etc.) This kind of sentence is a **complex sentence.**

    Run-on with comma splice: The Texas Rangers were master trackers, they provided information to the army.

    Correct: The Texas Rangers were master trackers **who** provided information to the army.

    Run-on: The river is high we have had heavy rains.

    Correct: The river is high **because** we have had heavy rains.

5. Turn one of the sentence parts into a phrase and combine it with the other sentence part.

    Run-on: Soo-Lin watched the snowflakes they were swirling and dancing.

    Correct: Soo-Lin watched the snowflakes swirling and dancing.

Study these ways of fixing fragments and run-on sentences. Notice that you must understand the meaning of a run-on sentence before you can decide which method will fix it.

For example, look back at the run-on sentence in 2, above. It was fixed by using the word *but* to connect the sentence parts. Using *and* or *or* would not have made as much sense.

Now look at the second run-on sentence in 4, above. It was fixed by using the word *because* to join the two sentence parts. The word *although* would not make sense here at all.

WARNING: This is a common trap on writing tests. Many wrong answer choices join sentence parts together with words that don't fit. A test might contain a run-on sentence like the one in 4 above: *The river is high we have had heavy rains.* Then it might ask you if the sentence can be fixed by writing *Although the river is high, we have had heavy rains.* This trap won't catch you if you pay attention to the meaning of what you read.

Finally, when you fix a run-on sentence by combining sentence parts, be sure that your new sentence is good, grammatical English. You can end up with an ungrammatical sentence if you're not careful.

For example, look back at the first run-on sentence in 3, above: *Suzanna volunteered to take tickets tonight last night she sold programs.* You could not fix it by combining the sentence parts this way: *Suzanna volunteered to take tickets tonight, last night selling programs.* This combination doesn't make sense. It doesn't mean what the original sentence meant.

▲ Practice

Rewrite each of the following to fix the run-on sentences. Follow the directions in parentheses and the examples above.

d. Test the alarm by pressing the button replace the battery if necessary. (Split into two sentences. Follow the example in 1, above.) _____

_____

e. Vincent wanted a snack he didn't have change for the machine. (Connect the sentence parts with one of the following conjunctions: *and, or, but,* or *for*—whichever makes sense. Follow the example in 2, above.) _____

_____

f. Our team is in green the visitors are in blue. (Use a semicolon to connect the sentence parts. Follow the example in 3, above.) _____

_____

g. We recently visited Guadalupe Mountains National Park, it is famous for its fossils. (Connect the sentence parts with a relative pronoun. If you're not sure what a relative pronoun is, look back at the first sentence in 4, above.)

_____

_____

h. Melvin stubbornly entered the pie-eating contest we advised him not to. (Connect the sentence parts with one of the following words: *although, until, before,* or *if*—whichever makes sense. Follow the second example in 4, above.)

_____

_____

   i. Anna stared sorrowfully at the vase it was lying broken on the floor. (Connect the sentence parts by turning the second part into a phrase. Follow the example in 5, above.)

_____

_____

Combining Sentences

You can combine sentences the same way that you combine sentence parts. You use exactly the same methods that you just used above in the Practice sections.

Sentences are most often combined when the second sentence repeats information that is already in the first. In the combination, the extra, repeated information is dropped.

> *Two sentences:* **I bathed my dog Sheba** yesterday. **I bathed her** in the lake.
>
> *Combined into one sentence:* I bathed my dog Sheba yesterday in the lake.
>
> *Another possible combination:* I bathed my dog Sheba in the lake yesterday.

Be careful when you combine sentences. Sometimes you may drop too much information. The following sentence is not a good combination of the example sentences above:

> *Bad combining:* Sheba got a bath yesterday in the lake.

This combination may look good at first. But it doesn't mean the same thing as the two original sentences. For one thing, it doesn't tell you who Sheba is! It also doesn't say who did the bathing.

Be careful of bad combinations like this. They are often used as wrong answer traps on the writing test.

Strategies and Tips

1. Be sure you know how to spot sentence fragments and run-on sentences. You will find the information and the **Strategies & Tips** that you need to know in the chapter before this one.

2. Be sure you understand all the ways of fixing fragments and run-ons and of combining sentences that are listed in this chapter.

3. Be careful of the following wrong answer traps. They often appear in the answer choices.

   A. Combining sentences in a way that does not make sense, or that does not mean the same as the original sentences.

   B. Combining sentences in a way that leaves out information or that changes what the original sentences say.

   C. Including wrong answer choices that contain fragments or run-on sentences.

28

Agreement

The form a word has in a sentence often depends on another word in the sentence. For example, we say *The dog barks*, not *The dog bark.* In this sentence, the form *barks* is said to **agree** with the word *dog*.

Agreement is an important area of English usage. This section of *The Writing Test* will review for you the important rules of agreement that may be tested on writing tests. There are two types of agreement that you need to know about:

A. **Subject-Verb Agreement.** Rules about how to make a verb agree with its subject.

B. **Pronoun-Antecedent Agreement.** Rules about how to make personal pronouns agree with the words they refer to or replace.

Agreement of Subject and Verb

GLOSSARY

First, here is a review of some terms you need to know. Look them over before you go on. You can refer to them whenever you need to.

NOUN. A noun is a word that names a person, place, thing, or idea.
Examples: friend   book   car   flower   piano   happiness

VERB. A verb is a word that shows action or a state of being.
Examples: talk   hop   know   fly   take   have   do   be

TENSE. Tense is a way of changing the verb form to show time. See the examples that follow on the next page.

GLOSSARY continues on the next page . . .

GLOSSARY (continued)

PRESENT TENSE. A present tense form is a verb form that shows present time.

Examples: talk *or* talks   hop *or* hops   take *or* takes
               have *or* has   am, is, *or* are

PAST TENSE. A past tense form is a verb form that shows past time.

Examples: talked   hopped   took   had   was *or* were

SUBJECT. The subject of a sentence is the word or group of words that tells who is doing the action of the sentence, or who the sentence is about.

Examples: *Sandra* is there.   The *milk* is cold.   *They* arrived early.
               Everyone clapped.

SINGULAR. A singular is a word form that is used when you are talking about only one of something.

Examples: table   robin   baby   goose   man   woman
               spaghetti   bravery

PLURAL. A plural is a word form that is used when you are talking about more than one of something. The plurals of many nouns are formed by adding the ending *-s.* A few nouns, however, form their plurals in other ways.

Examples: tables   robins   babies   geese   men   women
               (*Spaghetti* and *bravery* are examples of nouns that have
               no plural.)

PRONOUN. A pronoun is a word that takes the place of a noun. See the examples below.

PERSONAL PRONOUN. A personal pronoun is a word like *I, you, he, she, it,* or *they.* Personal pronouns often have different forms, depending on how they are used in a sentence: for example, the words *I, me, my,* and *mine* are all different forms of one personal pronoun.

INDEFINITE PRONOUNS. Indefinite pronouns are words like *someone, everybody, nothing,* etc.

PREPOSITIONAL PHRASE. A prepositional phrase is a group of words beginning with a preposition (words like *of, in, at, to, among,* etc.) and ending with a noun or pronoun.

Examples: of his   on the table   beside me   to school
               between us

1. NOUN + VERB. Verbs in the present tense have two forms. For example:

play/plays   march/marches

- When the subject is a *singular* noun, the verb must have the **-s** or the **-es** form.

    The fox play**s**.   The soldier march**es**.

- When the subject is a *plural* noun, the verb does *not* have the **-s** or **-es** ending.

    The foxes play.   The soldiers march.

- The verbs **have** and **do** have special forms for the present tense.

    has/have   does/do

    My cousin **has** a pet hamster.   Charlene **does** math well.

    My cousins **have** a pet hamster.   The girls **do** math well.

Choose the correct verb forms in parentheses.

    a. Nellie (create/creates) beautiful jewelry from walnut shells.

    b. That dog (dig/digs) in our garden whenever it (have/has) the chance.

    c. Few friends (is/are) as faithful as Freddy.

    d. Computers (help/helps) many people with disabilities.

2. PRONOUN + VERB. A verb in the present tense must agree with a pronoun subject, just as it must agree with a noun subject.

- When the subject is **he, she,** or **it,** the verb must have the **-s** or **-es** form.

    He watch**es** TV.   She swim**s** well.   It look**s** cloudy.

    She **has** a younger brother.

- With all other personal pronouns (**I, you, we,** and **they**) the verb does not have the **-s** or **-es** ending.

    I dislike eggplant.   You dance well.   We look silly.

    They have the same haircut.

Choose the correct verb form in parentheses.

    a. He never (give/gives) me enough time; it (make/makes) me angry.

    b. You (believe/believes) Joe, and she (believe/believes) Stacy.

    c. I (do/does) my exercises every day before I (go/goes) running.

    d. She (have/has) a nice voice, but I (sing/sings) like a frog.

3. NOUN + *BE*. The verb *be* has several forms. You must know them all, and know which ones to use with singular and plural subjects.

> *Present tense forms:* **am   is   are**
>
> *Past tense forms:* **was   were**

- When the subject is a *singular* noun, the verb *be* takes the form *is* (present tense) or *was* (past tense).

  > That sweater **is** pretty.
  >
  > The test **was** not hard.

- When the subject is a *plural* noun, the verb takes the form *are* (present tense) or *were* (past tense).

  > Those flowers **are** wilting.
  >
  > The clouds **were** closing in fast.

- Notice that the form *am* is never used with a noun subject.

IMPORTANT! The word *be* can never be used as a main verb or as a helping verb by itself.

> *Incorrect:* My sister be here. She be talking on the telephone.
>
> *Correct:* My sister is here. She is talking on the telephone.

Choose the correct forms:

    a. The park (am/is/are/be) a short drive from our home.

    b. The clouds (was/were) dark and threatening.

    c. My cousins (am/is/are/be) coming here for a visit.

    d. The cat (was/were) sleek and fat.

4. PRONOUN + *BE*. The following chart lists the correct forms of the word *be* with different pronouns. Any other uses will be considered incorrect on writing tests.

SINGULAR	
PRESENT TENSE	**PAST TENSE**
I am	I was
You are	You were
He/she/it is	He/she/it was

PLURAL	
PRESENT TENSE	PAST TENSE
We are	We were
You are	You were
They are	They were

Choose the correct forms:

  a. I (am/is/are/be) a member of that club.

  b. You (was/were) out when I called.

  c. We (am/is/are/be) ready for the big game.

  d. It (am/is/are/be) raining hard.

  e. They (was/were) sure they would be home on time.

  f. She (am/is/are/be) my closest friend.

  g. He (was/were) the star of the show.

5. COMPOUND SUBJECT + VERB. When the subject is a compound subject (two or more subjects joined by *and*), the verb is plural. That means it does not have the *-s* or *-es* ending.

  Patsy and I adore tacos.

  • Compound subjects take the plural verb forms *are, were, have,* and *do*.

    Sara and Beth **are** cheerleaders.
    Both he and I **have** ten-speed bikes.

Choose the correct forms:

  a. Her scarf and my hat (was/were) on the seat.

  b. Julio and Hank (does/do) a great comedy routine.

  c. Megan and her sister (sing/sings) alto in the chorus.

6. SUBJECT FOLLOWED BY A PREPOSITIONAL PHRASE.

Don't be fooled when a prepositional phrase comes between the subject and the verb. The verb agrees with the subject, not the noun in the phrase—even though the noun in the phrase is nearer the verb. You can be fooled when the subject is singular and the noun in the phrase is plural, as in the following examples.

One of the boys **is** (not *are*) absent.

The space between the buildings **was** (not *were*) narrow.

The dents in the fender **look** (not *looks*) fresh.

Choose the correct forms:

a. One of these books (is/are) overdue at the library.

b. One of the best things about Jack's teammates (is/are) their loyalty.

c. The milk in these glasses (have/has) a funny taste.

7. INDEFINITE PRONOUNS AND VERB AGREEMENT.

The pronouns known as indefinite pronouns can cause trouble with agreement. Some take a singular verb (with **-s** or **-es**). Others take a plural verb (no **-s** or **-es**). Still others may take either form. You should memorize the following lists. Questions about indefinite pronouns often turn up on tests.

The following are **singular** and take a singular verb. Notice that many of these end in **-one, -thing**, or **-body**:

one	everyone	someone	anyone	no one
everybody	somebody	anybody	nobody	
everything	something	anything	nothing	
each	either	neither		

Someone is coming.   Everybody is ready.   Nothing is wrong.   Either is OK.

The following are **plural** and take a plural verb:

both   several   many   few   a few   (This may look like a singular, but it isn't. It always takes a plural verb.)

Both need to be fixed.   Several have no names.   A few came before noon.

The following may be **either singular or plural.** Often the meaning gives the clue. Look at the examples:

all   some   any   most   none

Some (meaning "a certain amount") is singular:
Is the soup hot? Some **is.**

Some (meaning "some of them") is plural:
Are the tomatoes ripe? Some **are.**

Any (meaning "a certain amount") is singular:
I need some paper. **Is** there any in the drawer?

Any (meaning "some of them") can be either plural or singular:
Where are the kittens? **Are** any under the sofa? (when a plural answer is expected)
Where are the kittens? **Is** any of them under the sofa? (when the answer expected is "One" or "None")

All (meaning "everything" or "all of it") is singular:
All **is** quiet.

All (meaning "all of them") is plural:
I have many friends, but all **are** away right now.

Choose the correct forms:

a. Everybody (is/are) here now.

b. I want to take a bath. (Is, Are) there any hot water?

c. I want to take a bath. (Is, Are) there any clean towels?

d. Each (has/have) a toothbrush and a comb.

e. All but the slowest runners (has/have) finished the race.

f. Few (is/are) chosen for the highest honors.

Pronoun-Antecedent Agreement

The **antecedent** of a pronoun is the word that it refers to or replaces. In the sentence *Carol raised her hand,* the antecedent of the possessive pronoun *her* is *Carol.*

Most agreement problems with pronouns involve agreement in **number**.

8. AGREEMENT IN NUMBER. When the antecedent of a pronoun is singular, the pronoun must be singular, too. When the antecedent is plural, the pronoun must be plural.

The tiger bared **its** teeth (not *their* teeth).

Vernon and his sister defended **their** position. (not *his* position or *her* position.)

Most of the problems with agreement occur when the antecedent is an indefinite pronoun. And in many cases, the problem occurs when the antecedent is a singular indefinite pronoun like *each.* Look at the examples on the next page.

Incorrect: Each of the girls brought their own sleeping bag.
   (*Each* is singular; *their* is plural.)

Correct: **Each** of the girls brought **her** own sleeping bag.
   (*Each* is singular; so is *her*.)

Incorrect: Each of the boys took their lunch to the park.

Correct: **Each** of the boys took **his** lunch to the park.

Correct: **All** of the boys took **their** lunch to the park.

Study the examples and make sure you understand them. To review whether an indefinite pronoun is singular or plural, look at 7, above.

This is a fairly important usage point. It is often tested on writing tests.

Choose the correct forms:

   a. Either of the girls might have left (her, their) books behind.

   b. Some of the birds built (its nest/their nests) on that ledge.

   c. One of the choir members must have forgotten (their/his) music.

29

Verb Tenses and Verb Forms

In the previous section, you reviewed the forms that a verb may take in agreeing with the subject of a sentence. The form that a verb takes also depends on its tense and on whether it is used with a helping verb like *is* or *has*. These forms are reviewed in this section, together with hints on the types of questions that may be asked on writing tests.

GLOSSARY

To understand the usage rules in this section, you need to review the meanings of these terms.

PRESENT TENSE. The present tense of a verb is a form that is used when the action takes place in the present time. It is also used when the action is customary, repeated, or habitual.

> *Examples:* Dave **seems** sad.   I **wear** it.   Kay **feeds** the cat.
> Everyone **speaks**.   The lilac **is** in bloom.

PAST TENSE. The past tense of a verb is a form that is used when the action took place in the past.

> *Examples:* Dave **seemed** sad.   I **wore** it.   Kay **fed** the cat.
> Everyone **spoke**.   The lilac **was** in bloom.

PAST PARTICIPLE. The past participle of a verb is the form that follows the helping verb *have* or *has.* Sometimes it has the same form as the past tense. Sometimes it doesn't.

> *Examples:* Dave has **seemed** sad for a long time.
> I have **worn** it for a week.
> Kay has **fed** the cat.
> Everyone has **spoken**.
> The lilac has **been** in bloom since Sunday.

1. **REGULAR VERBS.** Most verbs form their past tense and past participle the same way—by adding the ending *-d* or *-ed* to the present tense. These verbs are called *regular verbs.* A regular verb's past participle has the same form as its past tense.

    smile, smil**ed**, smil**ed**   walk, walk**ed**, walk**ed**

2. **IRREGULAR VERBS.** A large number of very common verbs do *not* form their past tense and past participle by adding *-ed* to the present tense. They are called *irregular verbs.* They form the past tense and the past participle in different ways. Some keep the same spelling for all three forms. Some change the sound of the verb. Some add the ending *-en* to make the past participle. There is no one rule for them all. **Learn the ones on the opposite page!**

3. **VERB FORM TRAPS TO LOOK OUT FOR.** If a writing test has a question on verb tenses and forms, it may be on one of the following:

    A. With regular verbs, be sure you know when the past tense or the past participle is necessary, and be sure you know how to form both.

    Incorrect: Yesterday we hike four miles.
    Correct: Yesterday we hik**ed** four miles.

    Incorrect: I have already call you twice.
    Correct: I have already call**ed** you twice.

    Rewrite any underlined verb that has an incorrect form. Rewrite it in the correct form.

    a. Last summer we <u>camp</u> in Big Bend.

    b. I <u>returned</u> that purchase a week ago.

    c. During the 1800's, many people <u>move</u> west by wagon train.

    B. Don't form the past tense of an irregular verb by adding *-d* or *-ed.* You must know all the past tense forms of the common irregular verbs to avoid getting caught by this trap.

    Rewrite any underlined verb that has an incorrect form. Rewrite it in the correct form.

    a. I already <u>feeded</u> the dog.

    b. Amy <u>gived</u> me this game.

    c. He already <u>knowed</u> the answer.

    d. We <u>blowed</u> up a hundred balloons for the dance.

IRREGULAR VERBS

PRESENT TENSE	PAST TENSE	PAST PARTICIPLE (with *have*)
become	*became*	*become*
begin	*began*	*begun*
bet	*bet*	*bet*
blow	*blew*	*blown*
break	*broke*	*broken*
bring	*brought*	*brought* (not "brang" or "brung")
burst	*burst*	*burst* (not "busted")
buy	*bought*	*bought* (not "broughten")
catch	*caught*	*caught* (not "catched")
choose	*chose*	*chosen*
come	*came*	*come*
cut	*cut*	*cut*
dive	*dived, dove*	*dived*
do	*did*	*done*
eat	*ate*	*eaten*
fly	*flew*	*flown*
forget	*forgot*	*forgot, forgotten*
give	*gave*	*given*
go	*went*	*gone*
grow	*grew*	*grown* (not "growed")
hang (suspend)	*hung*	*hung*
BUT: *hang* (execute)	*hanged*	*hanged* [this is a regular verb]
have	*had*	*had*
hit	*hit*	*hit*
hurt	*hurt*	*hurt*
know	*knew*	*known* (not "knowed")
let	*let*	*let*
mean	*meant*	*meant*
ride	*rode*	*ridden*
ring	*rang*	*rung*
rise	*rose*	*risen*
run	*ran*	*run*
see	*saw*	*seen*
shine	*shone*	*shone*
sing	*sang*	*sung*
spring	*sprang, sprung*	*sprung*
stink	*stank*	*stunk*
strike	*struck*	*struck*
swim	*swam*	*swum*
take	*took*	*taken*
think	*thought*	*thought* (not "thunk")
throw	*threw*	*thrown* (not "throwed")
write	*wrote*	*written* (not "writ")

    e. Carlos <u>growed</u> four inches in the last three months.

    f. That garbage sure <u>smelled</u> up the place.

    g. Margo <u>fitted</u> the cap onto the top of the bottle.

C. Don't confuse the past tense and the past participle forms of irregular verbs. Again, you have to know all the irregular verb forms to avoid getting caught by this trap.

Rewrite any underlined verb that has an incorrect form. Rewrite it in the correct form.

    a. I have <u>rode</u> horses since I was little.

    b. He <u>come</u> into town wearing his best clothes.

    c. Jason has <u>brought</u> his sister with him.

    d. Consuelo has <u>chosen</u> to join the math club.

    e. The pitcher <u>threw</u> ten strikes in a row.

    f. She has <u>sang</u> with the chorus all year.

D. Be sure that the tense in question matches the sense of the sentence.

Rewrite any underlined verb that has an incorrect form. Rewrite it in the correct form.

    a. Since you left, the canary <u>escapes</u> and the cat ate it.

    b. If you stopped at the store, I hope you <u>pick</u> up a tube of toothpaste.

    c. I helped you whenever you <u>would have asked me.</u>

30

Pronoun Cases, Adjective and Adverb Forms, and Double Negatives

Pronoun Cases

GLOSSARY

Personal pronouns have different forms called *cases.* You should know the names of all these case forms and how they are used.

NOMINATIVE CASE. These forms are used as subjects of sentences.

Examples: I   you   he   she   it   they

OBJECTIVE CASE. These forms are used as objects of verbs and as objects of prepositions.

Examples: me   you   him   her   it   them

POSSESSIVE CASE. These forms are used to show possession or ownership.

Examples: my/mine   your/yours   his   her/hers   its   their/theirs

---

These are the most common traps involving pronoun cases that may appear on writing tests:

1. **SUBJECT FORMS.** Be sure that a pronoun subject of a sentence is in the nominative case.

> **They** are my favorite group. (not "Them's my favorite group.")

Usually the trouble comes with compound subjects.

> **Cara and I** saw that movie. (not "Cara and me saw that movie.")
>
> **He and she** are cousins. (not "Him and her are cousins.")

HINT: Here's a tip. Whenever you see a sentence where a pronoun is used as part of a compound subject, try it with one pronoun as the subject. You might think that "Cara and me saw that movie" was OK, but if you tested it using just one pronoun—"Me saw that movie"—you would know it was incorrect.

Choose the correct forms:

  a. Julia and (I/me) first met at camp.

  b. (Him/He) and Mark are wearing identical shirts.

  c. (Her/She) and Alan got the same answer.

2. **OBJECT FORMS.** Be sure that the pronoun object of a verb or a preposition is in the objective case. Again, most of the trouble here comes with compound objects.

> The teacher called on **her and me.** (not "The teacher called on she and I.")
>
> The experience taught **John and him** a lesson. (not "The experience taught John and he a lesson.")

Once again, test by using the pronoun alone. You might say "The experience taught John and he a lesson," but if you tested it using the pronoun alone—"The experience taught he a lesson"—you would know it was wrong.

Choose the correct forms:

  a. Trudi invited both (Jenna and I/Jenna and me).

  b. Let's keep this (between you and I/between you and me).

3. POSSESSIVE FORMS. Be sure that a pronoun in the possessive case has the correct form. Usually, the major problem is with spelling. The rule is that a possessive personal pronoun never has an apostrophe. The word *it's* (with an apostrophe) is not a possessive. It stands for *it is*.

> **its** eyes (not "it's eyes")   The book is **theirs.** (not "The book is their's.")

REMEMBER THIS:

> **its** = possessive of **it**
>
> **it's** = **it is**

However, indefinite pronouns *do* have an apostrophe in the possessive.

> everyone**'s** friend   no one**'s** idea   somebody**'s** car

Choose the correct forms:

    a. I am sorry (its/it's) so late.

    b. This must be (somebodys/somebody's) wallet.

    c. Myron is a good friend of (theirs/their's).

    d. My lunch was more expensive than (yours/your's).

Adjective and Adverb Forms

> ## GLOSSARY
>
> **ADJECTIVE.** An adjective is a word that modifies a noun (or, sometimes, a pronoun). That is, it describes or gives information about the noun or pronoun.
>
>   *Example:*   Ann's **new little** puppy is **cute** and **cuddly.**
>
> **ADVERB.** An adverb is a word that modifies a verb, an adjective, or another adverb.
>
>   *Examples*:   Evan ran **quickly** down the trail. (Adverb modifies the verb *ran*.)
>
>   It was an **unusually** clear day. (Adverb modifies the adjective *clear*.)
>
>   He poured the milk **quite** carefully. (Adverb modifies the adverb *carefully*.)
>
> *GLOSSARY continued on the next page . . .*

GLOSSARY (continued)

COMPARATIVE. The comparative is a special form taken by an adjective or adverb when two things are being compared.

Examples: Amy is **younger** than Nicole.
This book is **more interesting** than that one.
Jim behaves **more courteously** than Lester does.

SUPERLATIVE. The superlative is a form taken by an adjective or adverb when more than two things are being compared.

Examples: Anna is the **youngest** of my cousins.
This is the **most beautiful** painting here.
John's paper was the **most carefully** written.

These are the traps involving adjectives and adverbs that may appear on writing tests:

4. **CONFUSING ADJECTIVES WITH ADVERBS.** Don't mix up adjectives and adverbs. The most common error is to use an adjective form where an adverb is needed.

   Incorrect: He walked real quiet and soft.

   Correct: He walked **really quietly** and **softly**.

Here's a tip. Most adverbs have the ending *-ly.* In fact, one common way to form an adverb is to add an *-ly* to an adjective:

   easily   wisely   simply   stupidly
   vigorously   happily   sadly   normally

EXCEPTIONS: A few common adverbs do not end in *-ly:*

   fast   well   hard (The adverb *hardly* means something different.)

Some adverbs have two forms:

   slow *or* slowly   quick *or* quickly
   Go slow *or* Go slowly   Come quick *or* quickly

There are a few adjectives that end in *-ly.* Don't confuse them with adverbs.

   ugly   friendly   lovely   lively

Choose the correct forms:

    a. Chrissa visits (real/really) frequently.

    b. Jake threw the ball (hard/hardly).

    c. Morgan won (easy/easily).

    d. That is just her (normal/normally) way of talking.

    e. Megan works (hard/hardly).

5. CONFUSING *GOOD* AND *WELL*. It's easy to confuse the words *good* and *well*. Here are the rules for when each is used.

    A. *Good* is always an adjective.

        It's a good day today.   This is a good pen.
        Be good.   This ice cream tastes good.

    B. *Well* is sometimes an adjective meaning "healthy."

        I had a cold last week, but I'm well today.   You don't look well.

    C. *Well* is also the adverb form of *good* (answering the question "How?").

        You did that well.   Jeff drives well.

    D. Here are two places where *good* and *well* are often confused:

        I feel **good.** (This means I feel in a good mood, it's a good day, and I feel good about myself.)

        I feel **well.** (This means only that I feel healthy.)

Choose the correct forms:

    a. You look (good/well) with short hair.

    b. Juanita plays the flute (good/well).

    c. Lou is sick, but Ted is (good/well).

6. USING THE WRONG FORMS OF COMPARATIVES AND SUPERLATIVES. A wrong form of a comparative or a superlative is a common trap on a test. To avoid this trap, you must know how to form comparatives and superlatives correctly. Here are the rules:

    A. Adjectives and adverbs with one syllable usually form the comparative and superlative by adding *-er* or *-est* to the ordinary form of the word.

        old, old**er,** old**est**   fine, fin**er,** fin**est**   slow, slow**er,** slow**est**

B. Adjectives or adverbs with two or more syllables usually form the comparative and superlative by adding the words *more* or *most* before the adjective or adverb.

famous, **more** famous, **most** famous

delicate, **more** delicate, **most** delicate

C. Adjectives of two syllables ending in *-y* often are an exception to Rule B, above. They usually add *-er* or *-est*, like one-syllable adjectives.

funny, funni**er,** funni**est**

happy, happi**er,** happi**est**

Choose the correct forms:

   a. Casey is the (strongest/most strong) of all of us.

   b. Carolyn is (friendlier/more friendly) than her sister.

   c. We just had the (wonderfullest/most wonderful) vacation!

   d. I'd like to meet at an (earlier/more early) hour.

7. USING THE WRONG FORMS OF IRREGULAR COMPARATIVES AND SUPERLATIVES. Some adjectives and adverbs form their comparatives and superlatives in an irregular way. Tests often include these forms. *Learn this list!*

	COMPARATIVE	SUPERLATIVE
good	*better*	*best*
well	*better*	*best*
bad	*worse*	*worst*
ill	*worse*	*worst*
many	*more*	*most*
much	*more*	*most*
far	*farther* or *further*	*farthest* or *furthest*
little (adverb)	*less*	*least*

Choose the correct forms:

a. That was the (baddest/worst) test I ever took.

b. Today's lunch is much (gooder/better) than yesterday's.

c. I hope you're feeling (weller/better).

8. AVOIDING DOUBLE COMPARATIVES. If an adjective ends in *-er* or *-est*, don't use *more* or *most* in front of it. This usage error is called a *double comparative.*

Incorrect: Lincoln plays soccer more better than baseball.

Correct: Lincoln plays soccer better than baseball.

Choose the correct forms:

a. That's the (silliest/most silliest) trick you've ever pulled.

b. It is even (hotter/more hotter) today than yesterday.

c. Your problem is no (more harder/harder) to solve than mine.

Double Negatives

9. AVOIDING DOUBLE NEGATIVES. Words that give the idea of *no* or *not* are called negatives.

no   not   *the ending* -n't   never   nothing

no one   hardly   scarcely   barely

Don't use more than one negative in a simple sentence or in a clause. Using more than one is a usage error called a double negative.

Incorrect: He hasn't never done nothing mean. (This sentence actually contains three negatives: *-n't*, *never*, and *nothing*.)

Correct: He has**n't ever** done anything mean *or* He has **never** done anything mean.

Incorrect: I can't hardly hear you.

Correct: I can hardly hear you.

Rewrite each sentence to remove the double negatives.

a. People say George Washington never told no lie.

b. I couldn't scarcely lift that suitcase.

c. There wasn't nothing we could do about it.

31
Spelling

The spelling questions on writing tests will test you on words that students often misspell. (*Misspell* is one of them. See Rule 4.)

There are two ways for you to brush up on your spelling. One way is to learn some of the important rules of spelling. The other is to memorize lists of words that are often misspelled. In this section of **The Writing Test,** you can do both.

SPELLING RULES

1. *IE OR EI?* There's a famous spelling rhyme that you should memorize:

   Put *i* before *e* . . . (*Examples:* bel**ie**ve   gr**ie**f)

   Except after *c* . . . (*Examples:* re**cei**ve   de**cei**t)

   Or when sounded long *a*,

   as in *neighbor* and *weigh*.

   Choose the correct forms:

   recieve/receive   chief/cheif   piece/peice   sliegh/sleigh   relief/releif

2. **EXCEPTIONS TO THE RHYME.** There are several exceptions to the rule. Memorize the following two sentences—they contain the principal exceptions.

   Neither leisured foreign sheik seized their weird height as forfeit for their heifer's protein.

   A financier is a species of scientist.

   Unfortunately, the sentences don't make great sense—but they do the job.

   Choose the correct forms:

   wierd/weird   science/sceince   sieze/seize

3. **THE SOUND OF *K*.** At the beginning of a word, the sound of *k* is usually spelled with a *c*—unless it is followed by *e* or *i*.

Before an *e* or *i* the *k*-sound is usually spelled with a *k*.

    case   **c**an   **c**old   **c**ube   **c**areer

    kettle   **k**een   **k**iss   **k**indle (before *e* or *i*)

EXCEPTIONS: kangaroo   koala   kayak   karate

Choose the correct forms:

    collect/kollect   cennel/kennel   code/kode

    crude/krude   cilogram/kilogram

4. **PREFIXES.** This is the easiest spelling rule of all. When a prefix is added to a word, the spelling of the word doesn't change. The prefix doesn't double any letters. There is no spelling change at all.

    re + place = replace   mis + place = misplace   co + operate = cooperate

Choose the correct forms:

    mispell/misspell   inactive/innactive   disatisfied/dissatisfied

5. **SUFFIXES: AFTER FINAL *-E*.** There are three rules for you to remember here:

A. Drop the *-e* at the end of a word before adding a suffix beginning with a vowel (*a, e, i, o,* or *u*).

    pla**ce** + **-i**ng = pla**ci**ng   lik**e** + **-a**ble = lik**a**ble

B. Keep the *-e*, however, if you need it to preserve the *s*-sound of the letter *c* or the *j*-sound of the letter *g.*

    pea**ce** + **-a**ble = pea**cea**ble   mana**ge** + **-a**ble = man**age**able

Choose the correct forms:

    haveing/having   likeing/liking   traceable/tracable

C. Keep a final *-e* before adding a suffix beginning with a consonant.

    pla**ce** + **-m**ent = pla**ce**ment   mana**ge** + **-m**ent = mana**ge**ment

Choose the correct forms:

    hopful/hopeful   engagment/engagement

EXCEPTIONS: judgment   acknowledgment   argument
(Memorize these! They often appear on writing tests.)

6. **SUFFIXES: CHANGING FINAL -Y TO -I.** Again, there is more than one rule to remember:

Change a *-y* at the end of a word to *-i*—

- IF there is a consonant before the *-y*

- AND the suffix does <u>not</u> begin with *-i*.

   happy + -est = happiest   necessary + -ly = necessarily   try + -es = tries

BUT: toy + -s = toys   say + -s = says (vowel, not consonant, before the *-y*)

   try + -ing = trying   deny + -ing = denying (suffix begins with *-i*)

Choose the correct forms:

   fuzzyer/fuzzier   busyly/busily   enjoyable/enjoiable   drying/driing

7. **SUFFIXES: DOUBLING A FINAL CONSONANT.** This rule applies only to words that end with the letter combination consonant-vowel-consonant (*CVC*)—for example, words like d**rop**, cont**rol**, be**gin**, **shun,** etc. It does not apply to words that end with other letter combinations—for example, sh**ake** (*VCV*), la**ugh** (*VCC*), etc.

When a word ends *CVC*, double the final consonant before a suffix beginning with a vowel—

- IF the base word has only one syllable (*drop, shun,* etc.)

- OR IF the word is accented on the last syllable (*control, begin,* etc.)

   drop + -ing = dro**pp**ing   **shun** + -ed = shu**nn**ed (one syllable)

   cont**rol** + -ing = contro**ll**ed   be**gin** + -er = begi**nn**er (accent on last syllable)

BUT: **shake** + -ing = shaking (not *CVC*)

   travel + -ing = traveling (accent on first syllable, not last)

Choose the correct forms:

   shoping/shopping   edditing/editting   grining/grinning   burning/burnning

   admiting/admitting   offered/offerred   occured/occurred

8. **PLURALS: ADDING -S OR -ES.** The usual way of forming the plural of a noun is to add an *-s.* However, add *-es* to most nouns ending in *-s, -z, -sh, -ch,* or *-x.* (Notice that these words all end with the same general type of sound—a hissing or buzzing sound.)

   dog, do**gs**   shoe, shoe**s**   door, door**s**   bo**ss**, boss**es**

   eyela**sh**, eyelash**es**   por**ch**, porch**es**   fo**x**, fox**es**

Choose the correct forms:

wishs/wishes   trains/traines   taxs/taxes

9. **PLURALS: NOUNS ENDING IN -Y.** If a noun ends in a **-y**, the way you form the plural depends on the letter <u>before</u> the **-y**. See whether it's a vowel (**V**) or a consonant (**C**).

   A. *V + -y:* Just add **-s**.

   b**oy**, boy**s**   t**oy**, toy**s**   k**ey**, key**s**   monk**ey**, monkey**s**

   B. *C + -y:* Change **-y** to **-i** and add **-es**.
   ba**by**, bab**ies**   f**ly**, fl**ies**

   Choose the correct forms:

   pennys/pennies   skys/skies   allys/alleys   valleys/vallies

10. **PLURALS: WORDS ENDING IN -O.** Words ending in **-o** are like words ending in **-y**. The way you form the plural depends on whether the letter before the **-o** is a vowel or a consonant.

    A. *V + -o:* Just add **-s**.
    rat**io**, ratio**s**

    B. *C + -o:* Add **-es**.
    ec**ho**, echo**es**   pota**to**, potato**es**

    Choose the correct forms:

    rodeos/rodeoes   tomatos/tomatoes   heros/heroes

    EXCEPTIONS: Many words having to do with music (solos, pianos, sopranos, altos). Just add **-s**.

11. **PLURALS: WORDS ENDING IN -F AND -FE.** Words ending in **-f** or **-fe** form their plurals in two ways, depending on how the plurals are pronounced:

    A. If pronounced *fs*, just add an **-s**.
    roof, roo**fs**   chief, chie**fs**

    B. If pronounced *vz,* add **-es**.
    elf, el**ves**   knife, kni**ves**

    Choose the correct forms:

    shelfs/shelves   leafs/leaves   beliefs/believes (plural of *belief*)

SPELLING LISTS

The following group of spelling lists is made up of words that are often misspelled by students. Some may look easy—but all cause trouble.

There are more than 320 words here, which is a lot. To make things easier for you, they have been divided up into 16 smaller lists of 20 words each, plus a small list at the end.

Learn these words one list at a time. Here's a quick and fairly easy way to do it:

- Begin with List 1. Have someone read the words to you. Write each one down.

- Check your words. Mark the ones that you spelled wrong. **Important:** Also mark any words you weren't completely sure of, even if you got them right. (You may want someone else to check your list, too, to catch any misspellings you missed.)

- Study these words until you are sure you know how to spell them. Keep a separate record of them, and review them from time to time. They are problem words for you.

- Go to List 2 and repeat the procedure.

- Continue until you have studied all the lists. If you work on one list a day, you'll master all the words in less than a month.

LIST ONE	LIST TWO	LIST THREE
a lot	all right	beauty, beautiful
absence	already	because
accelerate	although	belief
acceptable	always	beneficial
accessible	among	benefited
accommodate	analyze	biscuit
accumulate	annually	bookkeeper
accustom	anonymous	bought
ache	anticipated	breathe
achievement	anxiety	bruise
acknowledgment	apologize	bureau
acquaintance	apparent	bury
acquire	appreciate	business
address	arctic	busy
adolescence, adolescent	arguing, argument	calendar
advantageous	arithmetic	cemetery
advice (noun)	arrangement	certainly
advise (verb), advisable	athlete	chocolate
advertisement	aunt	Christmas
against	balloon	colonel
aggressive	bargain	come, coming

LIST FOUR

committee
comparative
compliment (say nice
    things), complimented
concede
conceive
condemn
conscience
conscientious
conscious
controversy, controversial
correspondence
cough
could
council
country
criticize
cupboard
cylinder
defense
definitely

LIST FIVE

definition
dependent
descendant
describe
description
desert (a dry, sandy
    region)
desert (to leave)
dessert (sweet after a meal)
diligence
dining
disastrous
discipline
disease
dissatisfied
eighth
either
embarrass, embarrassed
endeavor
environment
especially

LIST SIX

exaggerate
exceed
exceedingly
except
exercise
exhausted
exhibit, exhibition
existence
experience
explanation
fascinate
favorite
February
fierce
foreign
formerly
forty
fourth
friend
gaiety
grammar

LIST SEVEN

guarantee
guard
guess
guidance
handkerchief
height
heir
heroes
hypocrite
immediately
incredible
independence, indepen-
    dent
interest
interrupt
irrelevant
it's (it is)
its (belonging to it)
jealousy
jewelry
judgment

LIST EIGHT

knowledgeable
laboratory
leisure
leisurely
license
lieutenant
listener
lose
luxury
magnificent
maneuver
marriage
mathematics
medicine
miniature
minute
miscellaneous
mischievous
mischief
misspell
morning

LIST NINE

mortgage
muscle
mysterious
necessary
neither
niece
ninth
no one
noticeable
nuclear
numerous
occasion
occurred, occurrence
occurring
often
omitting
opportunity
paid
parallel
paralyzed
particular

LIST TEN

peace (opposite of war)
people
performance
personal (belonging to a person)
personnel (workers)
petroleum
piece (a portion, a part)
pleasant
pneumonia
poison
politician
possession
possible
practical
prairie
prediction
preferred
prejudice
prepare

LIST ELEVEN

prescription
prestige
prevalent
primitive
principal (head of a school; main)
principle (a rule or a truth)
privilege
probably
procedure
proceed
profession
professor
prominent
protein
psychology
pursue
quiet (not noisy)
quite (fairly)
receipt

LIST TWELVE

receive
recommend
recommendation
referring
remember
renowned
repetition
resistance
restaurant
rhythm
right
rough
Saturday
saucer
schedule
scissors
seize
sense
separate
sergeant

LIST THIRTEEN

shining
silhouette
similar
sincerely
sophomore
specimen
stationary (not moving)
stationery (paper and pencils)
straight
studying
substantial
subtle
succeed
succession
supersede
surprise
surrounded
susceptible
their (belonging to them)
there (in that place)
they're (they are)

LIST FOURTEEN

technique
thorough
though
thought
through
to
too
tragedy
transferred
traveling
tremendous
trouble
Tuesday
two
tyranny
unnecessary
until
used
vacation
vacuum
valuable

LIST FIFTEEN

vegetable
vehicle
vengeance
very
villain
visible
weather
Wednesday
weigh
weight
were (past tense of are)
we're (we are)
wholly
withhold
woman
women
write, writing
wrote
you're (you are)
your (belonging to you)

32

Capitalization

These are the capitalization rules that you may be tested on:

1. COURTESY TITLES. Capitalize courtesy titles when used before the name of a person:

Mrs. Jackson	**M**r. O'Hara	**D**r. Rodriguez
Senator Scaggs	**M**s. Archuleta	**P**resident Bush

BUT: Jack is a **d**octor (title <u>after</u> the name)

Rewrite:

congressman weiss	mayor gomez	private bailey
princess beatrice	admiral crowe	aunt anita

2. LETTER OPENING. Capitalize the words in the opening line of a letter. This is the part called the *salutation,* and it usually begins with the word *Dear:*

Dear **L**uke,   **D**ear **M**s. **F**errero:

To **W**hom **I**t **M**ay **C**oncern: **D**ear **E**ditor:

Rewrite:

dear liz,   dear lieutenant ledbetter: dear mr. miller: dear sir:

3. LETTER CLOSING–FIRST WORD. Capitalize the first word only in a letter closing:

Yours sincerely,   **W**ith all good wishes,   **V**ery truly yours,

Rewrite:

sincerely yours,   yours truly,   love,

4. TITLES OF BOOKS, ETC. Capitalize the first word in the title of a book, story, song, movie, TV show, work of art, etc. Capitalize all other words in the title, too, <u>except</u>:

articles (the words **a, an,** and **the**)

short prepositions of four letters or less (**of, at, in, to, with,** etc.)

short conjunctions (**and, or, but, nor, for, yet, so**)

You capitalize one of these only if it is the first word in the title.

<u>**T**he **A**dventures of **T**om **S**awyer</u>   <u>**S**tar **T**rek</u>

<u>**T**o **K**ill a **M**ockingbird</u>   <u>**O**f **M**ice and **M**en</u>

Rewrite:

<u>the long valley</u>   <u>a night to remember</u>

<u>close encounters of the third kind</u>   <u>call of the wild</u>

5. PROPER NOUNS. Capitalize proper nouns. A proper noun is the name of a <u>spec-ific</u> person, place, or thing. Place names are particularly important. Capitalize names of countries, counties, cities and towns, streets and avenues, names of mountains, lakes, and oceans, buildings, bridges, etc.

Capitalize <u>all parts of the name</u>, except for words like *the* and *of* and *and*.

Study the examples carefully. You should understand every one of them. This is one of the most important capitalization rules, and it appears on almost every writing test.

A. PERSONS: **A**rsenio **H**all   **J**ulie **B**rown   **D**r. **M**artin **L**uther **K**ing, **J**r.

B. PLACES: **N**orth **A**merica   **U**nited **S**tates of **A**merica   **E**ngland   **A**tlantic **O**cean
Iowa   **D**allas **C**ounty   **S**an **A**ntonio   **C**entral **A**venue   **F**ourth **S**treet
Lake **S**uperior   **M**ount **E**verest   **P**leasantville **H**igh **S**chool
Golden **G**ate **B**ridge   the **A**lamo   the **D**eep **S**outh

(Be careful of one thing. Names of directions <u>don't</u> get capitalized: Texas is **w**est of Louisiana. The *Deep South* is capitalized because here *South* is not a direction; it's a place.)

C. LANGUAGES: **F**rench   **C**hinese   **E**nglish   **S**panish   **L**atin

D. NATIONALITIES AND ETHNIC GROUPS: **M**exicans   **C**ajuns
Comanches   **H**aitians   **P**alestinians   **I**sraelis   **A**frican-**A**mericans

(*Black* and *white* are not usually capitalized when they refer to races.)

E. CALENDAR NAMES AND NAMES OF HOLIDAYS: **M**onday   **A**pril

Independence **D**ay   **H**alloween   **V**alentine's **D**ay

(However, do not capitalize the names of seasons: **w**inter, **s**ummer, etc.)

F. WARS, BATTLES, AND HISTORICAL PERIODS: **W**orld **W**ar II

the **A**merican **R**evolution   the **R**enaissance   the **B**attle of **S**an **J**acinto

G. POLITICAL PARTIES: **R**epublicans   **S**ocialists   **T**ories   **L**abor

H. COMPANY AND ORGANIZATION NAMES: **G**eneral **M**otors   **M**obil **O**il **C**o.

Bank of **A**merica   **A**merican **E**xpress   **B**oy **S**couts of **A**merica

I. BRAND NAMES: **X**erox   **F**ord   **H**onda   **V**oyager   **I**vory **S**oap

Rewrite:

canada   black sea   gulf of mexico   randolph county   galveston bay

kodak   district of columbia   greek   tuesday   february

south american airlines   magnolia street   democrats   oldsmobile

pecos river   lincoln highway   san antonio   spring   cieneiga boulevard

east   harvey mudd college   new year's day   world war I   communists

Be careful! Four words in the list above are not capitalized. Two are little words, and two are separate items.

Rewrite the following name and address:

dr. augusta rucker

37 orchard street

paris, texas

6. **PROPER ADJECTIVES.** Capitalize proper adjectives. Proper adjectives are adjectives formed from proper nouns—usually from place names. Notice that the words they refer to are <u>not</u> capitalized:

Chinese cooking   **I**ndian summer   **F**rench poodle   **A**merican democracy

Rewrite:

brazilian diplomat   japanese industry   italian food

7. **DIRECT QUOTATIONS.** Capitalize the first word in a direct quotation, even when it is in the middle of a sentence:

> Marcy wailed, "**T**he dog is eating my homework."
>
> Her mother replied, "**Y**ou know he eats everything you leave on the floor."
>
> "**T**here's enough left to recopy, at least," Marcy sighed.

Rewrite:

> "how do you do the last problem?" Akbar asked. Jeff said, "divide by two and multiply by three."

Keep in mind that you do <u>not</u> capitalize the first word in an indirect quotation:

> Akbar asked Jeff how he should do the last problem. Jeff told him that he should divide by two and multiply by three.

IMPORTANT TIP: Many students can spot errors on multiple-choice tests of capitalization, but forget the rules when they write their own compositions. When you write something of your own, be sure to proofread it. Correct the capitalization mistakes just as you would on a test.

33
Punctuation

Here are the punctuation rules that you may be tested on:

END PUNCTUATION

1. PERIOD.

A. Put a period at the end of a sentence if the sentence is a statement, a command, or a request:

- *Statement:* There are nine planets.

  Grand Teton National Park is in northwestern Wyoming.

  Jessica has learned to do cartwheels.

- *Command or request:* Please sit down.   Give me a break.

B. Put a period at the end of an abbreviation.

Feb.   Mon.   U.S.   St.   Ave.

Rewrite:

Our street is being repaved   Turn off the light in the hall

You're late   Be here by six o'clock   We will meet again on Mon Apr 12

2. QUESTION MARK. Put a question mark at the end of a sentence that asks a question.

Where is my jacket?   Are there any onions?

When was the Battle of the Alamo?   What did the doctor say?

Rewrite:

Is Molly back yet   Who put that box there   What gives you that idea

How old is he   When did Illinois become a state

3. **EXCLAMATION MARK OR EXCLAMATION POINT.** Put an exclamation mark at the end of a statement, command, or expression of strong feeling.

   Look out!   Don't you dare!   Leave me alone!   What a jerk!   Ouch!

4. **EXCLAMATION MARK WITH *HOW* AND *WHAT*.** Put an exclamation mark at the end of certain expressions and sentences that begin with the words **how** or **what**.

   How hot it is!   What a glorious sunrise we're having!

   How handsome you look!   What an odd thing to think!

   Don't confuse this kind of sentence with a question.

   How hot is it?   What kind of day will it be?

   The meaning of the sentence will tell you whether to use an exclamation mark or a question mark.

   Rewrite:

   Stop   What a beautiful painting   You fool   How I love pizza

---

COMMA

5. **IN A SERIES.** In a series of three or more words, phrases, or clauses, put a comma between each member of the series:

   - *Words:* Texas, New Mexico, Arizona, and California all border on Mexico.
   - *Phrases:* Luis stormed down the stairs, out the door, and into the yard.
   - *Clauses:* We do not know who she is, where she came from, or why she is here.

   (Some writers leave out the comma before the conjunction. Don't worry—you won't be tested on this.)

   Rewrite:

   They went to France Belgium and Holland last summer.

   Ted looked up briefly shrugged his shoulders and returned to his reading.

   Mary cooked the roast Joan made the salad and Judy boiled the rice.

6. **BETWEEN INDEPENDENT CLAUSES.** Put a comma between two independent clauses joined by a coordinating conjunction. The comma goes before the conjunction.

- *Independent clauses* are clauses that could stand alone as complete sentences.
- *Coordinating conjunctions* are **and, but, or, nor, for, yet, so**. Memorize them!

> The concert was canceled, so we went to a movie.
>
> Helen works hard, but Maddy works harder.

Rewrite:

> I heard the phone but I was in the shower.
>
> Peter pitched the tent and Linda gathered firewood.

WARNING: Don't use a comma to separate two verb phrases. The sentence below needs no comma:

> Sharon sat down at the piano and began to play.

7. **BETWEEN CERTAIN ADJECTIVES.** Put a comma between adjectives—if you would use the word *and* between them instead of the comma.

> a warm, friendly person   a clear, cold, sunny morning

If the word *and* would not sound natural between the adjectives, don't put in a comma.

> a tall brick building   curly brown hair

Rewrite if necessary:

> a cute little puppy   a dark stormy night
>
> his first big break   this funny sad fascinating book

8. **TO SET OFF NONRESTRICTIVE PHRASES AND CLAUSES.** Use commas before and after nonessential ("nonrestrictive") phrases and clauses, which are not essential to the flow of the sentence.

- *Nonessential phrases:* Lucy, carrying her violin in one hand, vaulted onto the stage.

- *Nonessential clauses:* The mail, which is nearly always late, was early today.

Rewrite:

> Mitchell holding a fistful of coins approached the vending machines.
>
> The nearest machine which was labeled "Snacks" swallowed his money and gave him nothing.

WARNING: A common test trap is to put in one comma and leave out the other. Don't let this trap catch you!

9. TO SET OFF APPOSITIVES. Use commas to set off appositives. An *appositive* is a noun (plus any other words that describe or modify it) that stands next to another noun and gives additional information about it.

Alison Jones, my next-door neighbor, is a pianist.

Rewrite:

Joel's mother an ecologist will speak in the auditorium.

Our dinner chicken stew on a bed of rice was cold and gummy.

Razorbacks fierce wild hogs with hairy bodies are immune to snakebite.

The test a multiple-choice examination will be given Friday.

WARNING: This is another place where a test question can trap you by putting in one comma and leaving out the other. Remember, whenever an expression should be set off by two commas, you need to check that both commas are there (unless, of course, the expression is the first or last thing in the sentence).

10. AFTER THE OPENING OF A FRIENDLY LETTER. Put a comma after the opening of a friendly letter. (With a business letter you use a colon—see Rule 24.)

Dear Luisa,   Dear Mom,   Dear Uncle Stan,

Rewrite:

Dear Sheila   Dear Aunt Bea   My Darling

11. AFTER THE CLOSING OF A LETTER. Put a comma after the closing of a letter.

Yours sincerely,   All the best,

Rewrite:

Yours truly   Sincerely yours   With love

12. DATES. Put a comma between the day and year of a date.

January 28, 1994   Sept. 11, 1934

Rewrite:

May 1 1948   Apr. 19 1776

13. PLACE NAMES. Put a comma between the name of a city and a state or the name of a city and a country.

Lawrence, Kansas   Amarillo, Texas

Veracruz, Mexico   Rapid City, S. Dak.

Rewrite:

Jacksonville Florida   Garland Texas   Brussels Belgium   Bethel VT

14. BEFORE DIRECT QUOTATIONS. Put a comma before a direct quotation, after words that identify the speaker.

Sara shouted, "Toss me the rope."   I shouted back, "What rope?"

Rewrite:

The nurse asked "Who's next?"

Mr. Gilhooley responded "I believe I am."

(See also Rule 26 on where to place the quotation marks and Rule 7 in the section on Capitalization for how to capitalize a quote.)

15. TO SET OFF NOUNS OF ADDRESS. Use a comma to set off a person's name when he or she is being spoken to. (A noun used this way is called a *noun of address*.)

Aaron, do you know the answer?   Here's your change, Mr. Daly.

Listen to me, Buster, or you'll be sorry.

Rewrite:

If you can manage it Carrie I'd appreciate some help.

I'm sorry Bob.

Miss Adams I'd like you to meet my mother.

16. AFTER CERTAIN INTRODUCTORY WORDS. Use a comma after an introductory word that doesn't have a strong connection to the rest of the sentence.

Well, look who's here.   Yes, I know her.   Boy, that was fun.

Rewrite:

No I haven't seen your pen.   Yes I do.   Well first the rain has to stop.

17. AFTER TWO OR MORE INTRODUCTORY PREPOSITIONAL PHRASES.
Use a comma after a series of prepositional phrases that start a sentence.

> At the top of the mountain, we planted a flag.

> Before the beginning of recorded history, people lived in caves.

Rewrite:

> In a circle of white birches near the river we made our camp.

> Before the invention of the clock time was kept by the hourglass.

NOTE: After a <u>single</u> prepositional phrase at the beginning of a sentence, you don't usually need a comma. You may put one in, however, to avoid confusion or if the phrase is a very long one. And you also put one in if the phrase has a weak connection with the sentence as a whole (Rule 16.)

18. AFTER AN INTRODUCTORY PARTICIPIAL PHRASE. Put a comma after an introductory participial phrase.

A *participial phrase* is a phrase built around the verb form known as a *participle*. There are two kinds of participles you should be aware of:

- *present participles* (participles ending in *-ing*):

  eating   taking   loving   fooling

- *past participles* (the verb form that is often found after the helping verb *have* or *has*):

  eaten   taken   loved   fooled

Participles are words that are formed from verbs, but participial phrases are not part of the verb of a sentence. In most cases, a participial phrase acts something like a prepositional phrase.

> Whipping in the breeze, the proud flag caught the morning sun.

> Bent and broken, the bicycle lay in a corner of the garage.

> Given no chance to survive, he amazed his doctors with his speedy recovery.

> Singing softly, Lila arranged the flowers she had picked.

Rewrite:

> Having stood empty for many years the house began to fall down.

> Surprised at her remark Stephen stopped where he was.

> Towering over the other buildings the skyscraper cast a long shadow.

19. AFTER AN INTRODUCTORY DEPENDENT CLAUSE. Put a comma after a dependent clause that begins a sentence.

- A *dependent clause* is a clause with a subject and a verb, usually introduced by words like *if, because, although, after, before, when,* etc.

    After dinner was over**,** we went out for ice cream.

    If you finish your job**,** you can help with mine.

    Because it is raining**,** we have to cancel the picnic.

Rewrite:

When I signal throw me the ball.

After she arrived the party became livelier.

Whenever it snows Lucian insists on going sledding.

SEMICOLON

20. BETWEEN INDEPENDENT CLAUSES. Put a semicolon between two independent clauses that are not connected by coordinating conjunctions (see Rule 6, above).

The sun set**;** darkness covered the land.

Pierre L'Enfant designed the nation's capital**;** Benjamin Banneker made it happen.

Rewrite:

The ladder wobbled Lynn slipped and fell.

The trapeze artists flew high above the crowd everyone gasped in appreciation.

The pigeons flew up suddenly George ducked.

WARNING: A semicolon is often used to fix a run-on sentence. Refer to page 137 for more on the topic. You are likely to run into this usage on many writing tests.

21. BETWEEN CLAUSES CONNECTED WITH A WORD LIKE *HOWEVER.*
The following words are often used to connect two clauses:

    however   nevertheless   therefore   moreover   thus

When any of these words begins the second clause—

    —a semicolon goes before it, and

    —a comma goes after it.

We have tried hard; nevertheless, we have not succeeded.

I have all the necessary qualifications; therefore, I am running for president.

Rewrite:

We scanned the sky with our telescope however we could not find the comet.

Leo was not watching the conductor thus he missed his only cue.

APOSTROPHE

IMPORTANT: Apostrophes are punctuation marks that appear as part of a word. On many writing tests, however, a mistake in the use of an apostrophe is considered a mistake in <u>punctuation</u>, not a mistake in spelling.

22. IN POSSESSIVES. Use an apostrophe to form the possessives of nouns and indefinite pronouns.

- For singular nouns, add **'s**.

  a cat**'s** dish   a year**'s** time

  Jess**'s** answer   Mrs. Washington**'s** hat

- For plural nouns ending in **-s,** just add an apostrophe.

  the students**'** grades   the Andersons**'** car

- For plural nouns that <u>don't</u> end in **-s,** add **'s** (just like a singular noun).

  women**'s** coats   men**'s** shoes

- For indefinite pronouns, add **'s.**

  everyone**'s** rights   somebody**'s** mistake   no one**'s** fault

Write the possessives of:

boy   James   Dr. Hertz   members   the Smiths   someone

men   woman

WARNING: The possessives of personal pronouns do not contain apostrophes:

his   hers   its   theirs

Note the word ***its*** especially: there is no apostrophe for the possessive.

23. IN CONTRACTIONS. Put an apostrophe in a contraction in place of the letter or letters that are dropped.

      isn't   hasn't   doesn't   won't   couldn't (apostrophe in place of the *o* in *not*)

      I'm   you're   he's   she's   it's   they're   you've

Rewrite:

    havent   shouldnt   didnt   doesnt   Ive   theyre (for <u>they are</u>)

WARNING: Be careful of *it's* and *its*. Remember:

    Its is the possessive of *it.*

    It's is the contraction of *it is.*

COLON

24. AFTER THE BEGINNING OF A BUSINESS LETTER. Put a colon after the opening of a business letter. (With a friendly letter you use a comma—see Rule 10.)

    Dear Sir: Dear Mrs. Beebe: Dear Congressman Gomez:

Rewrite:

    Dear Dr. Roth   Dear Senator Mason   Dear Mr. President

25. TO INTRODUCE A LIST. A colon is often used to introduce a list of words or phrases.

    Her shopping cart contained these items: a can of tuna, a jar of pickles, a bunch of celery, and a quart of orange juice.

    Be sure to bring these supplies: a calculator, two sharpened pencils, an eraser, and scratch paper.

Rewrite:

    I would like these things for my birthday a personal tape player tapes a bicycle tickets to a rock concert and a dog. (Don't forget to put commas in this sentence, too. See Rule 5.)

QUOTATION MARKS

26. TO SET OFF A DIRECT QUOTATION. Put quotation marks before and after a direct quotation—that is, a quotation that repeats the exact words of a speaker or of a text.

> "I feel like a chicken sandwich," said Katy.
>
> "Really?" quipped Bob. "How does a chicken sandwich feel?"
>
> I'd like to know who said, "Laugh and the world laughs with you."

Rewrite:

> You're acting childish, said Lawanna.
>
> That's because I'm a child, answered Phil.

WARNING: When you take a writing test, watch out for quotation marks. It's a common trap to put in the first set and leave the second set out. Make sure you add the second set.

(See also Rule 14 on the use of commas to punctuate quotations, and Rule 7 of the section on *Capitalization* for how to capitalize a quotation.)

PART THREE

PRACTICE TESTS

A
Sentence Construction and Combination

Read the passage. Some sections are underlined. The underlined sections may be one of the following:

- Incomplete sentences
- Run-ons
- Correctly written sentences that should be combined
- Correctly written sentences that do not need to be rewritten

Choose the best way to write each underlined section. If the underlined section needs no change, mark **"D Correct as is."**

The name "Allen" has an important place in American comedy. George Burns and Gracie Allen were a famous comedy team. They started in vaudeville they later appeared in movies and on
(1)
television. People still enjoy reruns of their weekly show. Steve Allen is another comedian.
(2)
Steve Allen was one of the first television talk show hosts. His "man on the street" skits are considered classics of early television. Woody Allen is also a well-known comedian, actor, and director.
(3)
He has established his own unique style of offbeat humor.

---

1. **A** They started in vaudeville and later appeared in movies and on television.

    B They started in vaudeville; appeared later in movies and on television.

    C They started in vaudeville. Later appearing in movies and on television.

    D Correct as is

2. **A** Another comedian, Steve Allen, was one of the first television talk show hosts.

    B Because Steve Allen was another comedian, he was one of the first television talk show hosts.

    C Another comedian was named Steve Allen, but he was one of the first television talk show hosts.

    D Steve Allen was another of the first comedians to host television talk shows.

3. **A** Woody Allen is also a well-known comedian he is an actor and a director.

    B Woody Allen who is also a well-known comedian, actor, and director.

    C As well as Woody Allen, a well-known comedian, actor, and director.

    D Correct as is

B

Usage 1

Place a check mark (✔) before each of the following sentences that contains an error in usage and underline the incorrect word or words. Then write the correct form of the underlined word or words on the line that follows. (You don't have to do anything if the sentence is correct.)

1. Julio spoke real softly to us.

2. Those children plays well together.

3. Maria sang a song she had wrote.

4. Each has his own opinion.

5. Let's keep this between you and me.

6. You was late again this morning.

7. I knowed you wouldn't let me down.

8. She and Lindy are going camping together.

9. She and Jack make a good team.

10. We all jumped when the balloon burst.

11. I can't hardly stand to hear you say that.

12. You play the guitar very good.

13. Most of the group will be here, but a few isn't coming.

14. We have already talk to him.

15. I've just had the most funny experience of my life.

16. She is gone but not forgotten.

17. I hope everyone brought their sweaters.

18. They gave the prize to my brother and I.

19. Luis throwed me out at first base.

20. That squirrel has an avocado pit in it's teeth.

21. Our house has a new coat of paint.

22. Last year I was sick, but I've been good so far this year.

23. Are you feeling any weller today?

24. Most cats is pretty independent.

25. This vacation is even more better than the last one.

26. Neither interests me.

27. Yesterday he came in and asks for you.

28. I wish you could do that more quicker.

29. One of my favorite foods is noodles.

30. This is the most delicious cake I've ever eaten.

C

Usage 2

Usage is often tested in a format like this one.

Read the passage and choose the word or group of words that belongs in each space.

Dear Karla,

It has now been over two months since you moved away, but I still ____(1)____ you as much as ever. ____(2)____ think of you often and talk about all the good times we had together. Many of the students in your class last year ____(3)____ me for your new address. I've told them how much you like to receive letters!

I hope that you are making lots of new friends and that you are now feeling ____(4)____ to your new home and new school. Write soon and let me know how things have been going for you.

Your friend,

Laura

---

1. **A** would miss
    B had missed
    C miss
    D will be missing

2. **A** The other girls and I
    B Me and the other girls
    C Myself and the other girls
    D The other girls and me

3. **A** has asked
    B have asked
    C asks
    D was asking

4. **A** adjustable
    B adjustment
    C adjusting
    D adjusted

D

Capitalization

Place a check mark (✔) before each of the following sentences (or parts of a letter) that contains an error in capitalization, and underline any incorrect word or words. Then write the incorrect word or words correctly on the line that follows. (If the sentences have no capitalization errors, you don't have to do anything.)

A capitalization error may be of two kinds. Either a word should be capitalized, or a word has been capitalized wrongly.

1. Dear professor McCardle:

   _____

2. The principal asked, "what is your name?"

   _____

3. Have you ever read Only In America?

   _____

4. Most employers require a High School diploma.

   _____

5. It is hard to get good Mexican food in the East.

   _____

6. Nick ordered a tent from outdoor outfitters, inc.

   _____

7. Cindy's address is 341 Cumberland drive, Fort Worth, Texas.

   _____

8. Who will the democrats nominate next?

   _____

9. very truly yours,

   _____

10. Jessica announced, "According to the map, we are only a few miles West of the padre island national seashore."

   _____

   _____

E
Spelling

Place a check mark (✔) before any of the underlined words that are misspelled. Then write the correct spelling on the line that follows. (If the spelling is correct, you don't have to do anything.)

1. Circle this date on your calendar.

   _____

2. I sincerly hope you mean that.

   _____

3. The accident occured on Friday.

   _____

4. Use your best judgement.

   _____

5. Did you recieve an invitation to the party?

   _____

6. We spent our vacation traveling across Texas.

   _____

7. Try not to disappoint me.

   _____

8. What movie do you recommend?

   _____

9. That is terrible-tasting medecine.

   _____

10. I am hopping you can make it.

    _____

11. Please peel the potatos.

    _____

12. I don't believe we have met.

    _____

13. Snow covered the rooves of the town.

    _____

14. Sal has a bowl full of pennies.

    _____

15. That movie is definitely weird.

    _____

16. She and Kate are always argueing.

    _____

17. I would have prefered to stay home.

    _____

18. Your remark embarassed me.

    _____

19. Hector complained to the managment.

    _____

20. The house was visable in the distance.

    _____

21. They were attacked by a fierce tiger.

    _____

22. Mosquitoes are a big annoyance.

    _____

23. I often run errands for my nieghbor.

    _____

24. It is a priviledge to meet you.

    _____

25. Lem's conscience is bothering him.

    _____

F

Punctuation

Place a check mark (✔) before any of the following sentences (or parts of a letter) that contains an error in punctuation. Then put in the correct punctuation under the place where it should go. (If a sentence is correctly punctuated, you don't have to do anything.)

1. Carl breathed the fresh clean air.

2. The wind wailed; the house creaked and moaned.

3. Just what Carol, were you thinking of?

4. Give me ten minutes and I will explain everything.

5. Dear Assemblyman Kelleher,

6. Which of the states is the largest.

7. Yours very truly

8. Everyones' vote counts equally.

9. Morgan replied, "I haven't the slightest idea."

10. My uncle, who had the lead in this year's play, is a plumber.

11. In the top drawer of the desk in the far corner of the room Ellie May finally found a pencil.

12. Vermont, New Hampshire, and Maine are New England states.

13. Here is what we need: cups, plates, forks, and napkins.

14. Tanya, the guest of honor was the last one to arrive.

15. My dear Aunt Joan:

16. What a delicious dinner.

17. Chris moved here from Philadelphia Pennsylvania.

18. The sun glinted off the windows of the tall building

19. If you can't stand the heat get out of the kitchen.

20. I won't be home, however, you can call and leave a message.

21. Stop it, you creep!

22. "If you do your best, said Nan, "we will surely win."

23. Having been up since dawn, Lester decided to nap.

24. She was born on June 16 1979.

25. Yes I mean it.

G

Mechanics

Capitalization, Spelling, and Punctuation are often grouped together as "Mechanics" and tested together in a form like the one below.

Read the passage and decide which type of error, if any, appears in each underlined section.

> Rodeo fans will be gearing up for <u>the Sixth Annual travis county Rodeo</u> to be held all next week.
> (1)
> Bill and Peg Murray, <u>this year's rodeo champions</u> will lead the parade into the town square on
> (2)
> Monday. Following the opening <u>ceremonys in the arena</u>, rodeo riders will perform from 7:30 P.M. to
> (3)
> 9:00 P.M. <u>"Bring your ten-gallon hats and your boots and ride with us!" invites Peg. "We'll have a</u>
> (4)
> great time in the old West tonight!"

1. **A** Capitalization error
    B Spelling error
    C Punctuation error
    D No error

2. **A** Capitalization error
    B Spelling error
    C Punctuation error
    D No error

3. **A** Capitalization error
    B Spelling error
    C Punctuation error
    D No error

4. **A** Capitalization error
    B Spelling error
    C Punctuation error
    D No error

ANSWER KEY

PART ONE

*Most of the exercises in **Part One** of the book can be answered in more than one way. Answers are given only for certain exercises in the Critical Thinking lessons that begin **UNITS ONE** and **THREE**, where one answer is expected.*

UNIT ONE

1. CRITICAL THINKING: WAYS OF EXPRESSING AN OPINION

Exercise 2, *p. 18*

1. opinion
2. fact
3. opinion
4. fact
5. opinion
6. fact
7. opinion
8. fact
9. opinion
10. fact
11. fact
12. opinion
13. fact
14. opinion
15. opinion
16. opinion
17. fact
18. fact
19. opinion
20. fact
21. opinion
22. opinion
23. fact
24. fact
25. opinion

UNIT THREE

CRITICAL THINKING: WAYS OF BEING REASONABLE

Exercise 1, *p. 100*

1. b
2. a
3. a
4. a
5. a (but you can make a good case for b as well)

Exercise 4, *p. 103*

The following sentences are written in neutral language:
2, 4, 9, 10

PART TWO

26. SENTENCE CONSTRUCTION

Practice, *p. 133*

Fragments: a, c, e, f, h, k

Practice, *p. 134*

Run-ons: l, m, n

27. SENTENCE COMBINING

Practice, *p. 136*

Answers will vary.

Practice, *p. 138*

d. Test the alarm by pressing the button. Replace the battery if necessary.
e. Vincent wanted a snack, but he didn't have change for the machine.
f. Our team is in green; the visitors are in blue.
g. We recently visited Guadalupe Mountains National Park, which is famous for its fossils.
h. Melvin stubbornly entered the pie-eating contest, although we advised him not to.
i. Anna stared sorrowfully at the vase lying broken on the floor.

28. AGREEMENT

p. 143 (top)
a. creates
b. digs
c. are
d. help

p. 143 (bottom)
a. gives, makes
b. believe, believes
c. do, go
d. has, sing

p. 144
a. is
b. were
c. are
d. was

p. 145 (top)
a. am
b. were
c. are
d. is
e. were
f. is
g. was

p. 145 (bottom)
a. were
b. do
c. sing

p. 146
a. is
b. is
c. has

p. 147
a. is
b. is
c. Are
d. has
e. has
f. are

p. 148
a. her
b. their nests
c. his

29. VERB TENSES AND VERB FORMS

p. 150 (A)
a. camped
c. moved

p. 150 (B)
a. fed
b. gave
c. knew
d. blew
e. grew

page 152 (C)
a. ridden
b. came
f. sung

p. 152 (D)
a. escaped
b. picked
c. asked me

30. PRONOUN CASES, ETC.

p. 154 (top)
a. I
b. He
c. She

p. 154 (bottom)
a. Jenna and me
b. between you and me

p. 155
a. it's
b. somebody's
c. theirs
d. yours

p. 157 (top)
a. real
b. hard
c. easily
d. normal
e. hard

p. 157 (bottom)
a. good
b. well
c. well

page 158
a. strongest
b. friendlier
c. most wonderful
d. earlier

page 159 (top)
a. worst
b. better
c. better

p. 159 (middle)
a. silliest
b. hotter
c. harder

p. 159 (bottom)
a. People say George Washington never told a lie.
b. I could scarcely lift that suitcase.
c. There wasn't anything we could do about it.

31. SPELLING

1. receive, chief, piece, sleigh, relief
2. weird, science, sieze
3. collect, kennel, code, crude, kilogram
4. misspell, inactive, dissatisfied
5. having, liking, traceable hopeful, engagement
6. fuzzier, busily, enjoyable, drying
7. shopping, editing, grinning, burning admitting, offered, occurred
8. wishes, trains, taxes
9. pennies, skies, alleys, valleys
10. rodeos, tomatoes, heroes
11. shelves, leaves, beliefs

32. CAPITALIZATION

1. Congressman Weiss,
   Major Gomez,
   Private Bailey,
   Princess Beatrice,
   Admiral Crowe,
   Aunt Anita

2. Dear Liz,
   Dear Lieutenant Ledbetter:
   Dear Mr. Miller:
   Dear Sir:

3. Sincerely yours,
   Yours truly,
   Love,

4. **The Long Valley**
   A Night to Remember
   Close Encounters of the Third Kind
   Call of the Wild

5. Do not capitalize:
   <u>of</u> in Gulf of Mexico
   <u>of</u> in District of Columbia
   <u>spring</u>
   <u>east</u>

   Dr. Augusta Rucker
   37 Orchard Street
   Paris, Texas

6. Brazilian diplomat,
   Japanese industry,
   Italian food

7. "How do you do the last problem?" Akbar asked. Jeff said, "Divide by two and multiply by three."

33. PUNCTUATION

1. Our street is being repaved. Turn off the light in the hall. You're late. Be here by six o'clock. We will meet again on Mon. Apr. 12.
2. There should be a question mark at the end of each sentence.
4. There should be an exclamation mark at the end of each sentence.
5. They went to France, Belgium, and Holland last summer.
   Ted looked up briefly, shrugged his shoulders, and returned to his reading.
   Mary cooked the roast, Joan made the salad, and Judy boiled the rice.
6. I heard the phone, but I was in the shower.
   Peter pitched the tent, and Linda gathered firewood.
7. a cute little puppy
   a dark, stormy night
   his first big break
   this funny, sad, fascinating book
8. Mitchell, holding a fistful of coins, approached the vending machines.
   The nearest machine, which was labeled "Snacks," swallowed his money and gave him nothing.
9. Joel's mother, an ecologist, will speak in the auditorium.
   Our dinner, chicken stew on a bed of rice, was cold and gummy.
   Razorbacks, fierce wild hogs with hairy bodies, are immune to snakebite.
   The test, a multiple-choice examination, will be given Friday.
10. Dear Sheila,
    Dear Aunt Bea,
    My Darling,
11. Yours truly, Sincerely yours, With love,
12. May 1, 1948
    Apr. 19, 1776
13. Jacksonville, Florida
    Garland, Texas
    Brussels, Belgium
    Bethel, VT
14. The nurse asked, "Who's next?"
    Mr. Gilhooley responded, "I believe I am."
15. If you can manage it, Carrie, I'd appreciate some help.
    I'm sorry, Bob.
    Miss Adams, I'd like you to meet my mother.
16. No, I haven't seen your pen. Yes, I do. Well, first the rain has to stop.
17. In a circle of white birches near the river, we made our camp.
    Before the invention of the clock, time was kept by the hourglass.
18. Having stood empty for many years, the house began to fall down.
    Surprised at her remark, Stephen stopped where he was.
    Towering over the other buildings, the skyscraper cast a long shadow.
19. When I signal, throw me the ball.
    After she arrived, the party became livelier.
    Whenever it snows, Lucian insists on going sledding.
20. The ladder wobbled; Lynn slipped and fell.
    The trapeze artists flew high above the crowd; everyone gasped in appreciation.
    The pigeons flew up suddenly; George ducked.
21. We scanned the sky with our telescope; however, we could not find the comet.
    Leo was not watching the conductor; thus, he missed his only cue.
22. boy's   James's
    Dr. Hertz's   members'
    the Smiths'   someone's
    men's   women's
23. haven't   shouldn't
    didn't   doesn't
    I've   they're
24. Dear Dr. Roth:
    Dear Senator Mason:
    Dear Mr. President:
25. I would like these things for my birthday: a personal tape player, tapes, a bicycle, tickets to a rock concert, and a dog.
26. "You're acting childish," said Lawanna.
    "That's because I'm a child," answered Phil.

PART THREE

PRACTICE TESTS

TEST A

1. A
2. A
3. D

TEST B

1. real   really
2. plays   play
3. wrote   written
4. correct
5. correct
6. was   were
7. knowed   knew
8. correct
9. correct
10. correct
11. I can't hardly
    I can hardly / I can't
12. good   well
13. isn't   aren't
14. talk   talked
15. most funny funniest
16. correct
17. their sweaters
    his sweater
18. I   me
19. throwed   threw
20. it's   its
21. correct

22. <u>good</u>   well
23. <u>weller</u>   better
24. <u>is</u>   are
25. <u>more better</u>   better
26. correct
27. <u>asks</u>   asked
28. <u>more quicker</u>
    more quickly/quicker
29. correct
30. correct

TEST C

1. C
2. A
3. B
4. D

TEST D

1. professor   Professor
2. what   What
3. In   in
4. High School   high school
5. correct
6. outdoor outfitters, inc.
   Outdoor Outfitters, Inc.
7. drive   Drive
8. democrats   Democrats
9. very   Very
10. West   west
    padre island national
    seashore
    Padre Island National
    Seashore

TEST E

1. correct
2. sincerely
3. occurred
4. judgment
5. receive
6. correct
7. correct
8. correct
9. medicine
10. hoping
11. correct
12. correct
13. roofs
14. correct
15. correct
16. arguing
17. preferred
18. embarrassed
19. management
20. visible
21. correct
22. correct
23. neighbor
24. privilege
25. correct

TEST F

1. Carl breathed the fresh, clean air.
2. correct
3. Just what, Carol, were you thinking of?
4. Give me ten minutes, and I will explain everything.
5. correct
6. Which of the states is the largest?
7. Yours very truly,
8. Everyone's vote counts equally.
9. correct
10. correct
11. In the top drawer of the desk in the far corner of the room, Ellie May finally found a pencil.
12. correct
13. correct
14. Tanya, the guest of honor, was the last one to arrive.
15. My dear Aunt Joan,
16. What a delicious dinner!
17. Chris moved here from Philadelphia, Pennsylvania.
18. The sun glinted off the windows of the tall building.
19. If you can't stand the heat, get out of the kitchen.
20. I won't be home; however, you can call and leave a message.
21. correct
22. "If you do your best," said Nan, "we will surely win."
23. correct
24. She was born on June 16, 1979.
25. Yes, I mean it.

TEST G

1. A
2. C
3. B
4. D